Breaking into Cybersecurity:
A Guide to Launching Your Cyber Career
Second Edition (2026)

Rob Chubbuck

ISBN: 978-1-970952-05-6

DEDICATION

To the disciplined builders, the career strategists, and the professionals who choose responsibility over comfort—this book is for you.

Cybersecurity is not merely a technical field. It is a profession grounded in trust, risk management, and stewardship of digital infrastructure. Those who enter it accept the responsibility of protecting organizations, economies, and individuals in an increasingly complex world.

To my children, who remind me that the future we are securing is not abstract—it is personal. May you always pursue knowledge with courage and integrity.

To my wife, Maria, whose strength, encouragement, and steady belief in my work have made this journey possible. Your support is the quiet architecture behind every page written.

To my family, mentors, and leaders who instilled in me the values of discipline, resilience, and lifelong learning—your influence is embedded in everything I teach.

To every professional stepping into cybersecurity—this field rewards preparation, clarity of purpose, and execution. May this book serve not just as instruction, but as a framework for building a deliberate and meaningful career.

- Rob Chubbuck

ACKNOWLEDGMENTS

This book represents more than writing—it reflects years of teaching, mentoring, consulting, and learning alongside dedicated professionals.

First, to my wife, Maria—your patience during long evenings of drafting and revising, your steady encouragement, and your unwavering belief in this mission have been foundational. You are the constant that makes sustained work possible.

To my children, who remind me daily why the work of cybersecurity matters. The systems we secure today shape the opportunities of tomorrow.

To my family and mentors, whose example of work ethic and integrity shaped the way I approach both leadership and education. Your influence continues to guide my standards.

To the students, certification candidates, and professionals who have trusted me with their development—this second edition exists because of your questions, your drive to improve, and your commitment to excellence. Your pursuit of growth continues to refine and elevate this work.

To the broader cybersecurity community—analysts, engineers, auditors, architects, executives, and educators—thank you for upholding the standards of a profession built on responsibility and trust.

Cybersecurity is a collective effort. This book is one contribution to that larger mission.

— Rob Chubbuck

Preface

Breaking Into Cyber in a More Demanding Industry

Cybersecurity has matured.

The headlines are louder.
The attacks are more sophisticated.
The technology is more complex.
And the expectations are higher.

When earlier editions of this book were written, cybersecurity was widely described as a field with explosive demand and a massive workforce shortage. That was true — and in many ways, it still is. Organizations continue to struggle to secure expanding digital environments, protect sensitive data, and manage growing regulatory obligations.

But the market has changed.

This second edition reflects the evolving cybersecurity landscape, incorporating updates in cloud security, AI-driven threats, and modern hiring expectations. Employers today expect more than certification badges. They expect demonstrated competence. They expect familiarity with cloud platforms. They expect comfort with identity management. They expect candidates who can think critically about risk, not just configure tools.

At the same time, artificial intelligence has entered daily cybersecurity operations. AI assists with log triage, phishing detection, anomaly analysis, and automation of repetitive tasks. Entry-level work has not disappeared — but it has evolved. Professionals must now validate automated systems, interpret machine-generated findings, and supervise AI-assisted workflows.

This shift should not discourage you. It should focus you.

Cybersecurity is no longer about learning a tool.
It is about developing judgment.

It is about understanding:

- Why identity is the new perimeter
- Why cloud security is foundational, not optional
- Why risk communication matters as much as technical skill
- Why documentation and clarity distinguish professionals

The path into cybersecurity still exists. But it requires structure.

This book is not designed to promise shortcuts. It is designed to provide direction.

You will learn how to:

- Select the right cybersecurity lane based on your strengths
- Build practical experience before your first cyber job
- Translate prior career experience into security value
- Sequence certifications strategically
- Position yourself professionally
- Succeed in your first 90 days

Cybersecurity rewards consistency.
It rewards curiosity.
It rewards disciplined learning.

If you are willing to build skills deliberately, document your growth, and think like a security professional, there is space for you here.

Let's begin.

1 Cybersecurity as a Profession

Risk, Responsibility, and Strategic Opportunity

Cybersecurity is no longer an IT support function.

It is a board-level risk discipline that directly impacts revenue, regulatory exposure, operational continuity, shareholder confidence, and national infrastructure.

Organizations today operate in an environment of continuous digital threat. Ransomware disrupts hospitals. Supply chain compromises impact federal agencies. Cloud misconfigurations expose sensitive data. Artificial intelligence accelerates both defensive automation and adversarial sophistication. Regulatory scrutiny intensifies across healthcare, finance, defense, and critical infrastructure sectors.

Cybercrime now represents trillions of dollars in annual global economic impact.

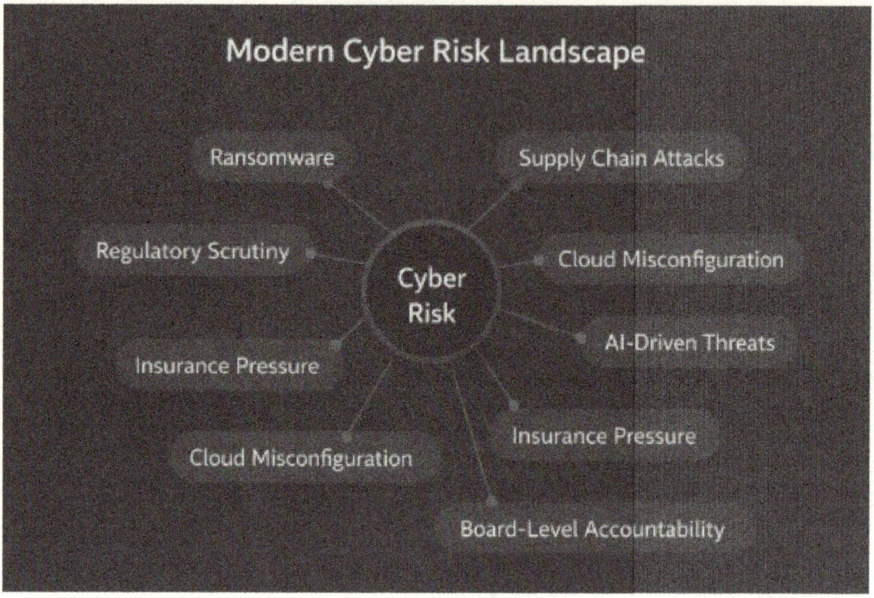

Figure 1. Modern Cyber Risk Landscape

Cyber risk is discussed in earnings calls. Executive leadership must quantify exposure with defensible metrics. Insurance carriers demand demonstrable control maturity. Audit scope continues to expand across regulated industries.

Enterprise security spending continues to scale because boards are now held accountable for measurable control maturity. The constraint is no longer "Does security matter?" but "Can the organization prove defensible risk reduction under scrutiny?"

In this environment, cybersecurity professionals are not optional.

They are strategic assets.

The Workforce Gap — and What It Really Means

Demand for cybersecurity professionals continues to outpace qualified supply, but the shortage is not merely numerical — it is competency-based.

Organizations are not merely seeking individuals who can run tools. They need professionals who can:

- Understand network and cloud architecture
- Interpret regulatory frameworks
- Translate technical findings into business impact
- Prioritize risk based on consequence
- Document controls for audit scrutiny
- Operate under pressure during incidents

Opportunity exists — preparation determines who captures it.

Cybersecurity rewards disciplined execution, not casual interest.

Cybersecurity Is the Discipline of Risk Management

At its foundation, cybersecurity is about managing digital risk.

Every security control exists because of identified risk:

- A firewall rule
- Multi-factor authentication
- Network segmentation
- Encryption standards
- Incident response procedures
- Audit logging requirements

Security is not about tools. It is about risk reduction.

Understanding this early distinguishes technicians from future leaders.

Qualitative vs. Quantitative Risk

Cyber risk can be evaluated in two primary ways:

- **Qualitative Risk** — High, Medium, Low assessments based on likelihood and impact
- **Quantitative Risk** — Estimated financial loss expectancy, probability modeling, business impact calculations

Boards and executives increasingly demand quantitative risk narratives. Insurance carriers demand measurable maturity. Regulators demand documented controls.

Security budgets are approved based on impact — not on technical preference.

If you understand risk economics, your value increases exponentially.

The AI Era Has Changed the Landscape

Artificial intelligence is transforming cybersecurity on both sides of the battlefield.

Attackers use AI for:

- Automated phishing campaigns
- Polymorphic malware
- Credential harvesting at scale
- Social engineering refinement

Defenders use AI for:

- Threat detection automation
- Behavioral anomaly detection
- Log correlation at scale
- Vulnerability prioritization

AI will not eliminate cybersecurity jobs.

It will increase demand for:

- Governance of AI systems
- Security architecture validation
- Risk modeling of AI applications
- Regulatory compliance oversight

Security professionals who understand AI governance and risk will be positioned at the forefront of the next decade.

Cybersecurity Career Taxonomy

Cybersecurity is not a single career path. It is a structured ecosystem of specialties.

Understanding these categories allows you to move intentionally.

Category	Primary Focus	Entry Certification	Intermediate	Advanced	Long-Term Roles
SOC / Defensive Security	Detection & Response	ISC2 CC	Security+ / Cloud+	CISSP	SOC Manager, IR Lead
Offensive Security	Adversary Simulation	Security+	eJPT / PNPT	OSCP	Red Team Lead
Cloud Security	Architecture & DevSecOps	Cloud+	AWS Security	CISSP	Cloud Security Architect
Governance, Risk & Compliance (GRC)	Risk & Regulatory Alignment	CC	Cloud+	CGRC → CCRMP	Director of Risk, CISO

Each path requires different cognitive strengths.

- Defensive roles require pattern recognition and rapid analysis.
- Offensive roles require creativity and technical depth.
- Cloud roles require architecture thinking.
- GRC roles require structured documentation and regulatory fluency.

Selecting a path early prevents certification drift and wasted effort.

Cybersecurity Is Recession-Resistant

Organizations may reduce discretionary technology projects during economic downturns.

They do not eliminate risk management.

Regulatory obligations remain. Insurance requirements remain. Incident response capability remains. Cloud infrastructure remains.

Security is now embedded in operational continuity.

Cybersecurity professionals who build structured expertise maintain long-term resilience.

Professional Standards and Ethical Responsibility

Cybersecurity professionals operate in environments of legal sensitivity and ethical obligation.

Security tools can disrupt systems. Penetration testing can cause unintended impact. Log access exposes sensitive information.

Ethical conduct is not optional. It is foundational.

Professional standards require:

- Responsible disclosure
- Legal authorization before testing
- Confidentiality discipline
- Accurate reporting
- Clear documentation

Reputation in cybersecurity is built slowly and damaged instantly.

Operate with integrity from day one.

Lessons From the Field

Over decades working across federal systems, enterprise migrations, regulatory audits, and incident response environments, one truth remains consistent:

Technology changes. Risk remains.

Organizations fail not because they lack tools — but because they lack structured implementation, documentation discipline, and risk prioritization.

The professionals who rise in this field are those who combine:

- Technical competence

- Structured thinking
- Documentation precision
- Communication clarity
- Continuous learning

Talent matters.

Discipline matters more.

The Reality: This Requires Deliberate Effort

Cybersecurity is achievable. It is not effortless.

You will need to:

- Master networking fundamentals
- Understand operating systems
- Study attack methodologies
- Build hands-on lab experience
- Practice structured documentation
- Develop professional communication skills

Expect complexity.

Competence is built through repetition.

Consistency replaces anxiety.

Your Strategic Starting Point

Before progressing, conduct a structured self-assessment.

1. Do I have foundational IT knowledge?
2. Which taxonomy category aligns with my strengths?
3. What certification can I complete within 90 days?
4. What weekly lab commitment will I maintain?
5. How will I document my progress professionally?

Clarity prevents drift.

Your 90-Day Execution Plan

Begin with measurable action.

Within 90 days:

- Select and begin one foundational certification (CC or Cloud+ depending on path).
- Build or configure a home lab (VirtualBox, cloud sandbox, or practice platform).
- Update your LinkedIn headline with cybersecurity positioning.
- Connect with 10 cybersecurity professionals.
- Draft a cybersecurity-focused resume version.
- Document one completed lab or mini-project.

Momentum builds identity.

The Commitment

Cybersecurity is not a short-term sprint.

It is a professional trajectory built through certification sequencing, lab execution, structured documentation, and disciplined networking.

If approached casually, progress will stall.

If approached strategically, transition into the field can occur faster than expected.

In **Chapter 2**, we will deconstruct cybersecurity career paths into executable entry strategies — certification sequencing, skill stacking, realistic timelines, and income progression — so you can design your path with precision rather than guesswork.

Clarity, sequencing, and disciplined execution create durable advantage.

Let's build yours deliberately.

2 Designing Your Cybersecurity Career Architecture

Cybersecurity does not reward randomness.

It rewards sequencing.

Many professionals enter this field with ambition but no structure. They collect certifications without direction. They pursue tools without understanding systems. They apply for roles misaligned with their current capability level. The result is frustration—not because the field is inaccessible, but because the approach lacks architecture.

You are not selecting a job. You are engineering a professional trajectory.

The Career Architecture Framework

A durable cybersecurity career is built through four deliberate phases:

1. **Foundation**
2. **Specialization**
3. **Credential Stacking**
4. **Market Positioning**

Each phase builds leverage. Skipping phases creates fragility. Mastering sequence creates acceleration.

Phase I: Foundation — Control the Fundamentals

Every cybersecurity role—offensive, defensive, cloud, governance, executive—rests on a common substrate:

- Networking
- Operating systems
- Identity and access management
- Basic scripting
- Security principles (CIA Triad, risk, controls)

Without this foundation, specialization becomes imitation.

A penetration tester without networking depth is a tool operator.
A GRC analyst without technical context becomes policy-only.
A cloud engineer without security fundamentals misconfigures at scale.

Your foundation determines your ceiling.

If you are entering from outside IT, your first objective is structural literacy:

- TCP/IP and the OSI model
- Authentication and authorization models
- Firewalls, IDS/IPS, and endpoint security
- Basic Linux and Windows administration

Certifications such as Security+ or ISC2 CC are not endpoints. They validate foundational comprehension. They do not create expertise.

Foundation precedes differentiation.

Phase II: Specialization — Select Your Domain of Leverage

After foundation, clarity becomes essential.

Cybersecurity is not one career. It is an ecosystem.

You must decide where you create value.

Specialization is not preference-based. It is constraint-based — determined by cognitive style, tolerance for ambiguity, communication orientation, and long-term earning model. Selecting a track based on trend or salary headlines creates friction. Alignment produces durability.

Below are four primary domains with long-term viability and compensation scalability:

1. Security Operations (SOC / Blue Team)

Focus:

- Threat detection
- Incident response
- Log analysis
- SIEM management
- EDR investigation

Core Tools:

- Splunk
- Microsoft Sentinel
- CrowdStrike
- Wireshark
- MITRE ATT&CK

This path develops operational awareness and investigative skill. It is high-pressure, fast-paced, and technically immersive.

It builds strong defensive instincts.

Case Example: Entry-Level SOC Analyst

A career changer with no prior IT background completed ISC2 CC and Security+ over four months while building a structured home lab focused on log analysis and basic SIEM usage. Within six months, he secured a Tier 1 SOC Analyst role at $68,000 annually in a mid-sized regional healthcare organization.

During his first year, he documented incident summaries, reduced false positives by refining alert logic, and gained exposure to cloud logging environments. Twelve months later, he transitioned to a Tier 2 Analyst role at $85,000 with expanded investigation responsibility.

The inflection point was not certification volume. It was disciplined documentation and structured reasoning under pressure.

2. Offensive Security (Red Team / Penetration Testing)

Focus:

- Vulnerability exploitation
- Network penetration testing
- Application security testing
- Adversary simulation

Core Knowledge:

- OWASP Top 10
- Active Directory attack paths
- Privilege escalation
- Post-exploitation techniques

This domain demands deep technical proficiency. It is not an entry-level shortcut. It requires mastery of networking, operating systems, and scripting.

Offensive credibility is earned through depth—not certifications alone.

3. Cloud Security Engineering

Focus:

- Securing AWS, Azure, or GCP environments
- Identity governance in cloud platforms
- Infrastructure as Code security
- Container and Kubernetes protection

This path has extraordinary growth velocity.

Organizations are migrating infrastructure faster than they are securing it.

Professionals who combine:

- Cloud architecture
- IAM discipline
- Logging and monitoring
- DevSecOps awareness

will command premium compensation.

Cloud security is not a trend. It is a structural shift.

4. Governance, Risk, and Compliance (GRC)

This domain is misunderstood and underestimated.

GRC is not paperwork. It is control architecture.

Governance roles sit closer to enterprise liability than most early-career candidates realize. They influence risk acceptance, audit outcomes, regulatory survivability, and executive reporting. As organizations mature, GRC authority moves upstream — from documenting controls to directing control strategy.

Figure 2. Risk Influence Escalation

Focus:

- Risk assessment lifecycle
- NIST 800-53 implementation
- ISO 27001 alignment
- SSP development
- POA&M management
- Control validation and audit readiness

This is the domain that translates technical controls into executive accountability.

As regulatory pressure increases and AI governance emerges, professionals who understand:

- Control frameworks
- Authorization processes
- Enterprise risk quantification

will operate at strategic levels of influence.

The CGRC and CCRMP certifications align specifically with this pathway—one focused on control implementation and authorization, the other on enterprise-level risk management leadership.

GRC is not passive work. It is structural risk governance.

Case Example: Governance Transition from Operations

A mid-career IT project manager transitioned into cybersecurity governance by pursuing CC followed by CGRC within nine months. She leveraged her documentation discipline and stakeholder communication experience to support NIST 800-53 control assessments in a federal contracting environment.

Her initial role as a Security Compliance Analyst began at $92,000 annually. Within two years—after supporting two Authority to Operate (ATO) cycles and leading internal audit preparation—she advanced to Senior GRC Analyst at $128,000.

Her acceleration was driven by control literacy, structured documentation, and executive-facing risk communication—not technical depth alone.

Phase III: Credential Stacking — Precision, Not Accumulation

Certifications are leverage instruments.

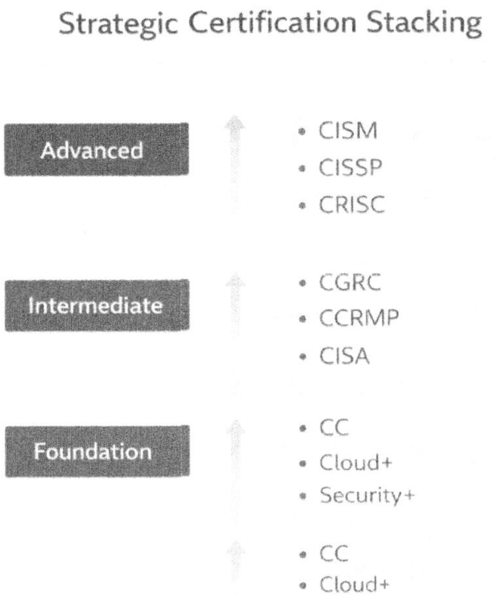

Figure 3. Strategic Certification Stacking

They are not trophies.

Random accumulation signals confusion. Strategic sequencing signals clarity.

Each credential must answer three questions:

1. Does this support my specialization?
2. Does this increase compensation tier eligibility?
3. Does this enhance credibility within my chosen domain?

Example of structured stacking:

Foundation Layer

- ISC2 CC or Security+

Intermediate Layer

- CySA+ (SOC)
- AWS Security Specialty (Cloud)
- CGRC (GRC)
- OSCP (Offensive)

Advanced Layer

- CISSP
- CISM
- CCRMP
- Specialized cloud architecture credentials

Every certification should create upward mobility.

If it does not, it is noise.

Phase IV: Market Positioning — Evidence of Capability

Capability is internal. Positioning is external.

The market rewards those who can demonstrate:

- Practical lab work
- Documented projects
- Incident narratives
- Control implementation examples
- Risk assessments performed
- Architecture diagrams created

Employers do not hire based solely on theoretical knowledge. They hire based on perceived risk reduction.

Your resume must communicate:

- Tools used
- Problems solved
- Impact delivered
- Metrics achieved

Your LinkedIn must reflect:

- Specialization alignment
- Consistent professional narrative
- Evidence of progression

Positioning converts preparation into opportunity.

Compensation Reality and Career Trajectory

Cybersecurity compensation scales with responsibility and impact.

Approximate market ranges (varies by region):

- Entry SOC Analyst: $55K–$75K
- Mid-Level Security Engineer: $90K–$120K
- Cloud Security Architect: $130K–$165K
- GRC Director: $140K–$180K+
- CISO (Enterprise): $180K–$300K+

Compensation varies by geography, organization size, security clearance requirements, and industry vertical.

Compensation follows scope.

Scope follows capability.

Cybersecurity Labor Market Economics

Cybersecurity is not just a technical discipline. It is a labor market shaped by economic forces — supply, demand, signaling, automation pressure, and organizational risk exposure.

Figure 4. Cybersecurity Labor Market Forces

Understanding these forces allows you to position yourself strategically rather than emotionally.

Supply vs. Demand: The Skills Gap Is Nuanced

You often hear that there is a "massive cybersecurity shortage." That statement is both true and misleading.

There is strong demand for experienced, high-signal professionals who can reduce measurable risk. There is not unlimited demand for entry-level candidates with undifferentiated resumes.

The labor market imbalance exists primarily at the mid-to-senior level, where professionals can:

- Lead risk assessments
- Architect secure systems

• Translate technical findings into executive impact
• Align security controls to regulatory requirements

Entry-level supply is increasing due to bootcamps, online certifications, and career changers. This creates hiring friction at the bottom of the market while leaving high-level roles persistently understaffed.

The lesson is clear: build toward structured capability, not just entry.

Credential Inflation: Why Baseline Certifications No Longer Differentiate

As more candidates enter the field, baseline certifications become normalized.

Security+, CC, and similar credentials often function as HR filters rather than differentiation tools. When thousands of applicants hold the same credential, it ceases to signal scarcity.

This phenomenon is called credential inflation.

Inflation does not make certifications worthless — it makes them foundational. The differentiator becomes:

• How you layer certifications
• How you align them to a career lane
• Whether you pair them with demonstrable outcomes

Stacking credentials without structured progression signals resume anxiety. Structured credential alignment signals strategic intent.

Markets reward the latter.

Automation and AI: The Compression of Tactical Roles

Automation and AI are reshaping cybersecurity roles.

SIEM platforms automate alert correlation.
Cloud providers auto-remediate misconfigurations.

AI tools generate incident summaries, scan code, and perform first-pass analysis.

This does not eliminate cybersecurity jobs. It compresses low-complexity tasks.

Tactical work that is repetitive, rules-based, and predictable becomes partially automated. Strategic reasoning, risk modeling, and cross-functional decision-making do not.

The professionals who remain valuable are those who:

- Interpret AI output
- Design control strategy
- Evaluate residual risk
- Communicate impact to leadership

Automation increases the premium on judgment.

Why Structured Reasoning Increases Lifetime Earning Ceiling

The highest-earning cybersecurity professionals are not those who memorize tools. They are those who think in structured frameworks.

Structured reasoning means:

- Understanding how controls map to risk
- Quantifying impact rather than describing symptoms
- Linking security investment to business continuity
- Anticipating regulatory implications

When you develop structured reasoning, you move from task execution to decision influence.

Decision influence increases compensation ceiling.

Technical execution caps early.
Risk translation scales upward.

A professional who can explain to a board why a $2M security investment prevents a $50M exposure operates in a different economic tier than one who simply configures a firewall rule.

This is why governance literacy, architecture thinking, and cross-functional fluency compound over time.

Cybersecurity labor economics reward scarcity, judgment, and strategic alignment.

If you understand how the market values capability — and you build accordingly — you will not merely enter cybersecurity.

You will position yourself to ascend within it.

Common Career Errors to Avoid

1. Pursuing penetration testing without foundational networking depth.
2. Ignoring documentation and communication skill development.
3. Avoiding cloud literacy.
4. Underestimating governance frameworks.
5. Collecting certifications without alignment.
6. Failing to quantify project outcomes.

These errors delay progression—not because they are catastrophic, but because they dilute focus.

Strategic Decision-Making in the AI Era

Artificial intelligence is reshaping security operations, threat detection, and governance.

Future-ready professionals must understand:

- AI model data leakage risks
- Prompt injection attacks
- Model poisoning
- AI governance compliance
- Responsible AI controls

Security will increasingly intersect with AI regulation and oversight.

Those who understand both risk frameworks and AI systems will operate at a strategic advantage.

AI will not eliminate cybersecurity roles. It will eliminate unstructured practitioners.

AI Era Professional Divide

Tool-Dependent Practitioner	Structured Risk Professional
• Executes predeined tasks	• Designs control strategy
• Relies heavily on automation outputs	• Interprets and validates AI outputs
• Focuses on tools rather than systems	• Thinks in systems and risk models
• Reacts to alerts	• Anticipates downstream impact
• Limited cross-functional visibility	• Communicates risk to leadership
• Career progression tied to technical tasks	• Career progression tied to decision influence

Figure 5. AI Era Profession Divide

As automation absorbs repetitive triage, scripted analysis, and template-driven documentation, the market will increasingly reward professionals who can think systemically, validate AI output, and make risk-based decisions under ambiguity. The advantage will shift from performing tasks to directing outcomes. Those who rely solely on tool familiarity will struggle. Those who combine structured reasoning with AI fluency will accelerate.

Deliberate Sequencing Creates Acceleration

Cybersecurity is not mastered in a year. It is constructed.

The professionals who accelerate are not necessarily the most brilliant. They are the most structured.

They:

- Build foundation.
- Choose specialization.
- Stack credentials with precision.
- Position themselves strategically.
- Adapt to emerging technology shifts.

Deliberate architecture produces velocity.

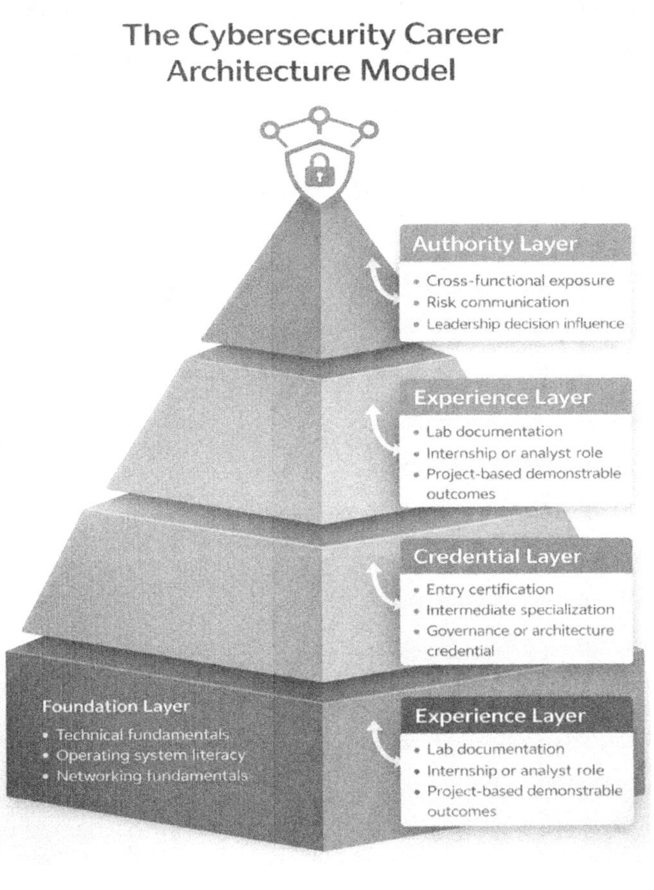

Figure 6. Cybersecurity Career Architecture Model

In the next chapter, we move from strategic architecture to tactical execution—building your 90-day action plan to convert structure into measurable forward momentum.

3 The 90-Day Execution Framework: Converting Strategy into Momentum

Clarity without execution is intellectual entertainment.

Career progression in cybersecurity is not determined by information consumption. It is determined by disciplined implementation.

You now understand:

- The structure of the industry
- The necessity of sequencing
- The specialization pathways available

You will not "try cybersecurity."
You will implement a 90-day operational plan.

The Execution Principle

Momentum compounds when action is structured.

Most professionals fail not from lack of intelligence, but from lack of cadence. They study inconsistently. They shift paths prematurely. They consume content without applying it. They wait for confidence before acting.

Confidence is produced by execution—not the other way around.

The next 90 days are not about mastery. They are about directional correction and disciplined momentum.

The 90-Day Structure

Figure 7. 90-Day Cybersecurity Execution Framework

This framework is divided into three 30-day phases:

1. **Foundation Reinforcement**
2. **Applied Skill Development**
3. **Market Activation**

Each phase has a distinct objective.

Do not merge them. Do not compress them. Do not skip them.

Phase I (Days 1–30): Reinforce Structural Competence

Objective: Remove technical fragility.

Regardless of background, assume your foundation requires strengthening.

Core Technical Reinforcement

You must demonstrate working understanding of:

- TCP/IP and packet flow
- DNS and DHCP mechanics
- Firewall rule logic
- Authentication vs authorization
- Windows and Linux user management
- Log file structure and interpretation

This is not academic review. It is operational familiarity.

Tactical Implementation

During these 30 days:

- Build or rebuild a home lab environment (VirtualBox, VMware, or cloud sandbox).
- Deploy at least one Windows and one Linux machine.
- Install and practice with:
    - Wireshark
    - Nmap
    - A basic SIEM trial (Splunk or equivalent)
- Capture packets.
- Analyze logs.
- Perform basic vulnerability scans.

If you cannot explain what you are observing, your foundation is incomplete.

Certification Alignment (If Applicable)

If pursuing Security+ or ISC2 CC:

- Study daily.
- Schedule the exam by Day 45.
- Do not "prepare indefinitely."

Deadlines create focus.

Phase II (Days 31–60): Specialization and Evidence Creation

Objective: Produce demonstrable proof of capability.

By Day 30, you should have chosen your specialization path. Phase II operationalizes it.

If You Chose Security Operations (SOC)

- Analyze simulated phishing samples.
- Create incident response flow documentation.
- Map one threat scenario to MITRE ATT&CK.
- Practice log correlation in SIEM.

Deliverable:
Write a short incident summary report as if presenting to leadership.

If You Chose Offensive Security

- Complete structured labs (TryHackMe, Hack The Box).
- Document one full attack path.
- Practice privilege escalation.
- Understand Active Directory attack vectors conceptually.

Deliverable:
Produce a penetration test-style findings summary with:

- Vulnerability description
- Exploitation method
- Risk rating
- Remediation recommendation

If You Chose Cloud Security

- Deploy a secure AWS or Azure environment.
- Configure IAM policies with least privilege.
- Enable logging (CloudTrail / Azure Monitor).
- Simulate misconfiguration and correct it.

Deliverable:
Create a short cloud security architecture summary explaining control decisions.

If You Chose GRC

- Conduct a mock risk assessment.
- Map 3–5 NIST 800-53 controls to a system.
- Draft a mini System Security Plan (SSP) excerpt.
- Create a basic POA&M entry.

Deliverable:
Produce a documented risk analysis with impact and likelihood scoring.

Phase II produces artifacts.

Artifacts create credibility.

Phase III (Days 61–90): Market Activation

Objective: Convert preparation into opportunity exposure.

Many professionals delay this phase out of insecurity. That delay compounds stagnation.

Activation begins before you feel "ready."

Resume Reconstruction

Your resume must now reflect:

- Tools used
- Labs completed
- Controls implemented
- Reports written
- Quantifiable improvements

Weak:

"Studied cybersecurity fundamentals."

Strong:

"Configured and monitored SIEM alerts in simulated enterprise environment; reduced false positives by refining rule logic."

LinkedIn Positioning

Update:

- Headline aligned to specialization
- Skills reflecting real tools used
- Project descriptions
- Professional summary emphasizing impact

Recruiters search by keywords. Position accordingly.

Application Cadence

Establish weekly rhythm:

- Minimum 5 targeted applications per week.
- Customization for each role.
- Networking outreach to 2 professionals weekly.

Not generic volume. Targeted exposure.

Application strategy should be asymmetric. Prioritize roles where your artifacts directly map to the job requirements — lab documentation, reports, control narratives, or incident summaries. Precision reduces interview friction more than volume increases probability.

Interview Preparation

You must be able to:

- Explain your lab environment clearly.
- Describe one technical problem you solved.
- Articulate risk in business language.
- Discuss AI-era security considerations.

If you cannot explain your own work coherently, revisit Phase II.

Performance Metrics for the 90-Day Framework

At Day 90, you should be able to answer "yes" to the following:

- Can I explain packet flow without hesitation?
- Have I built and operated a lab?
- Can I describe a full incident scenario?
- Have I written at least one professional-style report?
- Have I applied to positions aligned with my specialization?
- Have I scheduled or completed at least one certification exam?

If not, the issue is not capability—it is consistency.

Time Discipline and Cognitive Load Management

Cybersecurity requires sustained intellectual effort.

Recommended cadence:

- 60–90 minutes daily minimum
- One focused technical block
- One documentation or review block
- Weekly consolidation review

Avoid passive learning cycles (endless videos, no implementation).

Execution must exceed consumption.

The Compounding Effect of Structured Action

Most professionals overestimate what they can accomplish in a week and underestimate what disciplined execution produces in three months.

In 90 days, you can:

- Transform foundational weakness into operational confidence.
- Build a demonstrable portfolio.

- Reposition your professional narrative.
- Enter active job pipelines.
- Establish credibility within a specialization.

This framework produces measurable outcomes when implemented with discipline.

It is structured momentum.

The Difference Between Interest and Commitment

Interest studies when convenient.
Commitment executes when scheduled.

Cybersecurity rewards structure.

The professionals who advance are not those who wait for ideal conditions. They are those who implement under imperfect circumstances.

Strategic Continuity

The next chapter transitions from execution to competitive differentiation—how to stand out in a saturated applicant pool and build asymmetric advantage in an AI-accelerated industry.

The next decade of cybersecurity will be defined not by tool mastery, but by governance maturity, AI oversight, and enterprise risk fluency.

Structure determines entry.
Execution determines trajectory.
Influence determines legacy.

4 Competitive Difference: Building Asymmetric Advantage in Cybersecurity

There is a moment in every cybersecurity career when technical competence is no longer enough.

You may have earned certifications.
You may have built a lab.
You may have secured an entry-level role.

Yet you notice something.

Some professionals move quickly.
Others plateau.

The difference is rarely intelligence.
It is differentiation.

Cybersecurity is no longer an obscure niche profession. It is a globally recognized, heavily marketed, rapidly expanding field. Bootcamps promise rapid entry. Certifications are widely accessible. AI tools assist with scripting, log interpretation, and even vulnerability analysis.

The barrier to entry has lowered.

The barrier to advancement has not.

Advancement requires differentiation.

The Credential Illusion

Early in your career, credentials create momentum. They validate foundational competence and reduce hiring friction. But credentials have a shelf life.

As certification volume increases across the market, individual signaling value decreases proportionally.

When everyone has Security+, it is no longer a differentiator.
When many have CISSP, it becomes table stakes.
When cloud certifications are widespread, they no longer distinguish by themselves.

Organizations do not ultimately reward certificates. They reward capability that reduces organizational risk.

There are two professional identities in cybersecurity:

1. The credential holder
2. The risk reducer

Credential holders explain what they studied.
Risk reducers explain what they stabilized, prevented, or improved.

Advancement belongs to the second group.

Depth: Moving Beyond Tool Familiarity

Modern cybersecurity tools are powerful and accessible. AI-enhanced platforms can suggest mitigation steps. Automated scanners generate reports in minutes.

The danger is mistaking tool operation for expertise.

Depth is revealed when you can:

- Explain why a vulnerability exists—not just that it was detected.

- Describe how an attacker might chain multiple weaknesses together.
- Identify trade-offs between usability, cost, and security.
- Anticipate secondary impacts of mitigation decisions.

Consider a common scenario:

A misconfigured cloud storage bucket exposes sensitive data.

A novice response:

"We closed public access."

A differentiated response:

"We eliminated public access, audited IAM permissions for lateral exposure, implemented bucket-level logging, and adjusted our infrastructure-as-code templates to prevent recurrence."

The difference is systemic thinking.

Depth is not about memorizing more controls.
It is about understanding systems as interconnected risk surfaces.

Documentation: The Discipline of Serious Professionals

As you advance, one reality becomes increasingly clear:

Cybersecurity is traceable decision-making.

Executives make decisions based on documented evidence. Auditors validate compliance through documented controls. Incident response teams reconstruct timelines through documented events.

If you cannot document your thinking, your influence will be limited.

Documentation is not administrative overhead. It is strategic leverage.

You should become comfortable producing:

- Risk assessments with impact analysis.
- Control rationales aligned to frameworks.
- Architecture diagrams explaining trust boundaries.
- Incident narratives that show cause, containment, and prevention.

Professionals who document rigorously rise into leadership because documentation demonstrates structured reasoning.

It reveals not just what you did—but how you think.

Decision-Making Fluency: Translating Technical Action into Business Impact

Many technically strong professionals stall because they speak only in technical language.

Organizations do not fund firewalls. They fund risk reduction.

Every technical action must be translatable into:

- Financial exposure reduction
- Operational continuity
- Regulatory compliance alignment
- Brand protection

If you isolate a compromised endpoint, you did not merely "remove malware." You preserved operational continuity and reduced potential financial liability.

If you implement multi-factor authentication, you did not "improve login security." You reduced credential compromise probability and regulatory risk.

This shift in language changes how you are perceived.

Technician.
Engineer.
Advisor.

Advisors advance faster.

Communication Precision: The Hidden Career Multiplier

Cybersecurity operates under pressure. Breaches generate urgency. Compliance audits create deadlines. Executive briefings demand clarity.

In these environments, imprecise communication creates friction.

Differentiated professionals:

- Summarize complex issues in structured formats.
- Provide decision options—not just problems.
- Distinguish between urgent and important.
- Eliminate unnecessary jargon when speaking to leadership.

Precision does not mean oversimplification. It means clarity without distortion.

If you can explain zero-trust architecture to a non-technical executive in two minutes without sacrificing accuracy, you possess both mastery and influence.

Communication is not a soft skill in cybersecurity.

It is a force multiplier.

Technology Foresight: Operating Ahead of Industry Drift

Cybersecurity evolves faster than most professions.

Cloud adoption accelerated dramatically in the past decade.
AI integration is accelerating now.

Differentiation requires awareness beyond your current job description.

Emerging areas include:

- AI model governance and validation
- Prompt injection risk mitigation

- Data leakage via large language models
- Automated compliance tooling
- Infrastructure-as-Code security enforcement
- Continuous authorization frameworks

The professional who ignores AI governance today will be reactive tomorrow.

The professional who studies it now will advise leadership later.

You do not need to become an AI engineer.

But you must understand how AI changes attack surfaces, control expectations, and regulatory oversight.

Future influence belongs to those who anticipate—not react.

Portfolio as Strategic Evidence

Resumes describe claims.

Portfolios demonstrate reasoning.

Within your first year of structured effort, you should possess artifacts that reflect:

- An incident investigation summary.
- A cloud security configuration explanation.
- A mapped NIST control implementation.
- A quantified risk analysis.
- A redacted architectural diagram.

These documents change interviews from theoretical to analytical.

When asked how you approach risk, you can show.

When asked how you structure investigations, you can demonstrate.

Evidence compresses doubt.

Strategic Networking: Influence Without Desperation

Networking is often misunderstood as transactional outreach.

Strategic networking is intellectual visibility.

It includes:

- Participating in professional discussions.
- Contributing insight—not noise.
- Sharing lessons learned from structured lab work.
- Asking informed questions.

The objective is not immediate employment.

It is long-term positioning.

The cybersecurity community observes seriousness.
Consistency builds recognition.

Influence accumulates gradually.

The AI Compression Effect

Artificial intelligence is compressing the time required to perform routine tasks:

- Script generation
- Log parsing
- Initial vulnerability triage
- Research synthesis

This compression creates a paradox.

Entry-level technical barriers decrease.
Strategic reasoning requirements increase.

If AI can produce code, your value shifts to evaluating it.
If AI can generate reports, your value shifts to validating and

contextualizing them.
If AI can summarize logs, your value shifts to interpreting systemic risk.

The differentiated professional understands that AI is an amplifier—not a replacement.

Human judgment remains decisive in ambiguity.

Avoiding the Plateau

Many cybersecurity professionals plateau between years three and seven.

Why?

- They stop documenting growth.
- They remain tool-dependent.
- They avoid leadership responsibility.
- They neglect governance literacy.
- They disengage from emerging technologies.

Acceleration requires deliberate discomfort.

It requires expanding beyond current expertise.

The Asymmetric Advantage Principle

Asymmetric advantage in cybersecurity arises when you combine:

- Technical competence
- Governance literacy
- Communication precision
- AI awareness
- Structured documentation

Most professionals develop one or two of these.

Few develop all five.

Those who do become indispensable.

Strategic Continuity

Execution earns entry.
Differentiation earns acceleration.

In the next chapter, we shift from acceleration to sustainability—how to build a cybersecurity career that compounds over decades without burnout or obsolescence.

Because advancement is not the final objective.

Durability is.

5 Leveraging Your Legacy Experience

Many professionals assume transitioning into cybersecurity requires starting over. In reality, effective transitions compound existing capability rather than replace it.

Cybersecurity organizations do not only hire technical operators. They hire investigators, auditors, risk analysts, communicators, trainers, project managers, and engineers. The differentiator is not whether you have prior security experience — it is whether you can clearly translate your background into security-relevant value.

The objective is positioning, not reinvention.

Understanding Transferable Capital

Your prior career gave you three forms of capital:

1. Technical or domain knowledge
2. Decision-making experience
3. Professional maturity

Hiring managers assess career changers primarily on perceived risk. They ask:

- Can this candidate operate in a structured environment?
- Can they analyze problems?

- Can they communicate clearly?
- Can they be trusted with responsibility?

Your legacy experience answers these questions — if framed properly.

Transitioning from IT, Networking, or Helpdesk

If you come from IT support, networking, system administration, or development, you already possess foundational knowledge that many entry-level security candidates lack.

Common transition paths include:

- Helpdesk → Security Analyst
- Network Engineer → Security Engineer
- System Administrator → Cloud Security Engineer
- Developer → Application Security

Your troubleshooting background translates directly into:

- Log analysis
- Vulnerability remediation
- Patch management
- Identity and access configuration
- Incident triage

To strengthen positioning:

- Take ownership of security-related tasks in your current role.
- Build lab environments that simulate logging and detection.
- Document configuration decisions and risk implications.
- Pursue foundational security certifications aligned with your level.

Security is layered on top of infrastructure knowledge. If you understand systems, you already understand part of security.

Transitioning from Non-Technical Backgrounds

Cybersecurity also relies heavily on governance, risk management, compliance, auditing, and training functions.

Professionals from these backgrounds often transition successfully:

- Law enforcement → Digital forensics, incident response coordination
- Finance → Risk management, fraud analysis, compliance
- Legal → Governance, privacy, regulatory alignment
- Project management → Security program management
- Education → Security awareness, training development

Security teams need individuals who understand regulatory interpretation, documentation discipline, process design, and stakeholder communication.

The key is not becoming deeply technical overnight. The key is:

- Learning foundational security concepts
- Understanding common frameworks (NIST, ISO, SOC 2, HIPAA, etc.)
- Demonstrating structured analytical thinking

Identifying Your Transferable Skills

Regardless of industry, cybersecurity roles consistently value:

- Structured problem-solving
- Risk evaluation
- Clear documentation
- Attention to detail
- Stakeholder communication
- Policy interpretation
- Process improvement

Instead of asking, "Do I have cybersecurity experience?" ask:

"What security-relevant problems have I already solved?"

For example:

- Fraud detection is risk detection.
- Audit preparation is control validation.
- Investigations are incident response analysis.
- Compliance documentation is governance discipline.

Security teams need these capabilities.

Case Example: Non-IT Career Pivot

A former law enforcement investigator transitioned into cybersecurity with no formal IT background. He focused on structured upskilling: CC certification, foundational networking study, and documented incident simulation exercises. Within eight months, he secured a junior incident response coordination role at $72,000 annually.

His investigative background translated directly into timeline reconstruction, report writing, and evidence handling. Within three years, after earning CySA+ and expanding into threat intelligence analysis, his compensation increased to $105,000.

The pivot succeeded because he reframed investigation as incident response—not because he reinvented his identity.

Positioning Your Experience on a Resume

Translation is critical.

Hiring managers scan resumes quickly. They look for signals that reduce uncertainty.

Instead of listing prior responsibilities generically, emphasize security-adjacent actions.

Example:

Instead of:
"Managed Windows servers and provided technical support."

Write:
"Implemented access control policies, applied security patches, and ensured adherence to internal security standards for Windows server environments."

Instead of:
"Led cross-functional projects."

Write:
"Led compliance initiatives aligning operational processes with regulatory and internal control requirements."

This is not exaggeration. It is contextualization.

Bridging Knowledge Gaps Strategically

If you lack technical security exposure, focus on structured upskilling rather than scattered study.

Effective steps include:

- Completing role-aligned labs (defensive, cloud, governance, etc.)
- Studying foundational frameworks and terminology
- Earning an entry-level certification that validates baseline knowledge
- Documenting applied exercises and simulated scenarios

Avoid chasing credentials without context. Certifications are credibility markers — they are not substitutes for demonstrated capability.

How Hiring Managers Evaluate Career Changers

Hiring managers typically evaluate career transition candidates on three dimensions:

1. Demonstrated effort (labs, coursework, certifications)
2. Relevance of transferable skills
3. Professional maturity and communication ability

A well-positioned candidate with structured evidence often outperforms a purely technical candidate who lacks communication and discipline.

Legacy experience becomes an advantage when it demonstrates reliability and decision-making.

Final Thoughts

You are not abandoning your past career — you are reframing it.

Cybersecurity is a multidisciplinary field that rewards professionals who bring domain knowledge, structured thinking, and applied skill. By aligning your prior experience with security responsibilities and filling targeted knowledge gaps, you reduce the risk perception that often blocks career transitions.

In the next chapter, we will examine how certifications fit into this strategy — and how to choose them deliberately rather than reactively.

6 Certifications That Can Jumpstart Your Career

Cybersecurity certifications can strengthen your career trajectory — but they are not shortcuts.

In today's competitive hiring environment, certifications serve three primary purposes:

1. They help your resume pass screening filters.
2. They validate structured knowledge.
3. They signal professional commitment.

They do not guarantee interviews. They do not replace hands-on experience. And they do not automatically differentiate you from other candidates.

Certifications must be used strategically.

Are Certifications Necessary?

Not always — but often helpful.

Many organizations, especially in regulated or government-aligned environments, require or strongly prefer certifications. In other cases, certifications serve as screening mechanisms when employers receive large volumes of applications.

For early-career professionals and career changers, certifications reduce perceived hiring risk. They demonstrate that you have studied core security concepts and understand industry terminology.

However, certifications should support your target role — not substitute for experience or direction.

Certification Strategy by Career Stage and Role

Rather than grouping certifications by difficulty alone, it is more useful to think in terms of career stage and role alignment.

Certifications should build upon one another and form a coherent progression.

Foundational Certifications (Establishing Baseline Knowledge)

These certifications validate core cybersecurity principles and terminology.

ISC2 Certified in Cybersecurity (CC)

CC is designed for newcomers and career changers. It covers:

- Security principles
- Access control fundamentals
- Security operations basics
- Risk and governance concepts

CC is an excellent starting point for individuals entering cybersecurity from other industries or exploring the field for the first time.

CompTIA Security+

Security+ remains one of the most widely recognized entry-level cybersecurity certifications.

It covers:

- Risk management
- Cryptography
- Network security
- Incident response
- Security architecture

Currently, Security+ is often considered a baseline credential. Many candidates have it. It helps pass HR filters but does not independently differentiate you.

CompTIA Cloud+

Cloud+ bridges infrastructure and security. It focuses on:

- Virtualization
- Hybrid cloud environments
- Cloud networking
- Availability and resilience
- Secure configuration concepts

Cloud+ is increasingly valuable because modern enterprise environments are hybrid or cloud-native.

Infrastructure literacy is now a competitive advantage.

Role-Aligned Certification Pathways

Certifications should reflect your intended career lane. Below are structured examples aligned to modern hiring expectations.

SOC / Operations-Oriented Track (Cloud-Aware Defense)

Example Path:
CC → Cloud+ → CySA+ or GCIH

This pathway builds layered capability:

- CC establishes security fundamentals.
- Cloud+ develops infrastructure and cloud understanding.
- CySA+ or GCIH strengthens detection and incident response skills.

Modern SOC teams monitor:

- Cloud service logs
- Identity and access events
- SaaS environments
- Hybrid infrastructure

SOC analysts who understand cloud architecture and virtualization are more effective in real-world environments.

Cloud+ strengthens defensive literacy beyond traditional network-only thinking.

Governance, Risk, and Compliance (GRC) Track

Example Path:
CC → Cloud+ → CGRC → CCRMP

This pathway builds structured risk and compliance depth:

- CC provides foundational security knowledge.
- Cloud+ ensures infrastructure and cloud awareness.
- CGRC formalizes governance, RMF, and control alignment expertise.
- CCRMP strengthens applied risk management methodology.

Why Governance Careers Scale Faster in Compensation

Governance careers tend to scale more rapidly in compensation because they sit at the intersection of security, law, finance, and executive decision-making. Technical roles protect systems; governance roles influence budgets, risk tolerance, and regulatory posture. Organizations are willing to pay more for professionals who can quantify risk exposure, justify control investments, and communicate business impact to leadership.

As regulatory requirements increase and cyber risk becomes a board-level concern, governance professionals become strategically indispensable. A single effective governance leader can reduce regulatory penalties, prevent audit findings, and influence multimillion-dollar risk decisions. That level of organizational impact directly correlates to higher compensation bands.

In short, governance roles are compensated not only for technical knowledge, but for strategic influence and risk accountability.In regulated and federal environments, governance professionals must understand both frameworks and the systems they govern.

Cloud+ ensures that GRC professionals understand modern architectures.
CGRC and CCRMP reinforce structured risk thinking and program implementation.

This pathway is particularly strong for candidates targeting:

- Federal contracting
- NIST-based programs
- Healthcare and regulated industries
- FedRAMP-aligned environments

Infrastructure literacy combined with governance specialization creates strong positioning.

Technical Specialization Tracks

After foundational certifications, candidates may specialize further.

Defensive / Threat Detection

- CySA+
- GIAC GCIH
- SIEM platform certifications

These focus on:

- Log analysis
- Threat detection
- Incident response workflows

Offensive / Penetration Testing

- PenTest+
- OSCP

CEH remains widely recognized by HR departments, but many technical hiring managers prefer hands-on certifications or documented lab experience.

OSCP is rigorous and requires significant preparation. It should be pursued deliberately, not casually.

Cloud Security Specialization

- AWS Security Specialty
- Azure Security Engineer Associate
- CCSP (requires documented experience)

Cloud security continues to grow, but advanced cloud certifications require real-world exposure to be credible.

Certifications That Are Losing Standalone Impact

The hiring environment has shifted.

Certifications alone are rarely sufficient.

Security+ without applied projects does not differentiate.
CEH without hands-on proof carries limited technical weight.
Bootcamp completion without documentation is often ignored.

Certifications must now be paired with:

- Home lab documentation
- GitHub repositories
- Simulated scenario writeups
- Applied projects

Evidence matters more than titles.

When Not to Pursue Another Certification

Do not pursue additional certifications if:

- You cannot connect them to your target role.
- You are avoiding skill application.
- You are stacking credentials without progression.

A certification without applied practice becomes resume decoration.

Effective Certification Preparation

To prepare effectively:

- Review official exam objectives first.
- Study concepts, not memorized answers.
- Build practical labs aligned to the certification domain.
- Practice scenario-based thinking.
- Apply knowledge to simulated enterprise cases.

Employers quickly detect purely theoretical knowledge.

Strategic Reality

Certifications reduce hiring friction.

They do not replace demonstrated skill, structured reasoning, communication clarity, or professional maturity.

The strongest candidates combine:

1. A role-aligned certification pathway
2. Applied proof of capability
3. Clear professional positioning

That combination creates credibility.

Final Thoughts

Certifications are tools. Use them deliberately.

Choose credentials that:

• Align with your target lane
• Build progressively
• Complement hands-on skill development
• Strengthen your professional narrative

Certifications should support your strategy — not define it.

In the next chapter, we will focus on how to present your skills, certifications, and experience effectively on your resume and in interviews.

7 Resume Writing for Cybersecurity Roles

Your resume is not a biography.
It is a strategic positioning document.

In cybersecurity hiring, recruiters often spend less than 30 seconds scanning a resume before deciding whether to continue reading.

The goal is clarity, alignment, and credibility.

This chapter focuses on strategy — not formatting tricks.

Understanding How Cybersecurity Resumes Are Evaluated

Resumes are typically reviewed in three stages:

1. Automated screening (ATS or AI tools)
2. Recruiter scan
3. Hiring manager technical review

To pass all three:

• Your resume must reflect the language of the target role.
• Your experience must appear relevant immediately.
• Your claims must feel credible and supported.

Generic resumes fail because they try to apply to everything.

Focused resumes succeed because they target one lane.

Choose Your Target Role First

Before writing your resume, answer this:

Am I targeting:
• SOC Analyst?
• Cloud Security?
• GRC?
• Penetration testing?
• Compliance?

Your resume should not try to appeal to every cybersecurity discipline.

A SOC resume looks different from a GRC resume.

Alignment increases credibility.

Recommended Resume Structure (Early Career)

For candidates with limited formal cybersecurity experience:

1. Professional Summary (3–4 lines maximum)
2. Certifications
3. Technical Skills
4. Projects / Labs
5. Professional Experience
6. Education

Certifications and skills should appear above unrelated work history.

This ensures recruiters see your security positioning immediately.

Writing a Strong Professional Summary

Avoid generic statements like:

"Motivated cybersecurity professional seeking opportunities."

Instead, use positioning language:

"Entry-level cybersecurity professional with foundational certification (CC, Cloud+) and hands-on experience in cloud lab environments, identity configuration, and security monitoring. Focused on SOC and cloud-aware defense roles."

Specificity builds confidence.

Crafting a Resume Without Formal Cybersecurity Experience

If you do not have a cybersecurity job yet, your resume must emphasize:

- Applied lab environments
- Documented simulations
- Security-related responsibilities in prior roles
- Structured certification progression

Do not simply list:

"Completed TryHackMe rooms."

Instead:

"Built and documented a cloud-based lab environment simulating hybrid enterprise infrastructure. Performed log analysis, IAM configuration, and vulnerability assessments."

Frame projects as applied scenarios — not hobby participation.

Moving Beyond Generic Bullet Points

Hiring managers look for:

- Scope
- Tools
- Environment
- Decision impact

Even if you cannot quantify with percentages, you can demonstrate complexity.

Weak:
• Monitored network traffic.

Stronger:
• Analyzed authentication and network logs using SIEM tools in a simulated hybrid cloud environment to identify anomalous login behavior.

Weak:
• Configured security settings.

Stronger:
• Implemented access control policies and multi-factor authentication within a Windows Server lab environment to simulate enterprise identity management practices.

Depth matters more than buzzwords.

Using Keywords the Right Way

Modern ATS systems evaluate contextual relevance.

Instead of stuffing keywords, mirror job architecture.

If the job description emphasizes:

• Identity and access management
• Cloud logging
• NIST compliance

Your resume should reflect:

• IAM configuration
• Cloud lab security
• Familiarity with NIST control structures

Do not include tools you have never used.
Inflated resumes fail during interviews.

How to Position Certifications

Certifications should:

- Appear prominently
- Be listed chronologically
- Support your target lane

Example:

Certifications:
- ISC2 Certified in Cybersecurity (CC)
- CompTIA Cloud+
- CGRC (In Progress)

This tells a story.

Random stacking does not.

Technical Skills Section Strategy

Group skills logically:

Security & Monitoring:
- SIEM concepts
- Log analysis
- Incident triage

Cloud & Infrastructure:
- AWS (IAM, EC2, S3 basics)
- Virtualization
- Hybrid architecture

Governance & Compliance:
- NIST 800-53 familiarity
- Risk assessment concepts

Clustering shows intentional development.

What Hiring Managers Ignore

Avoid:

- Overly long objective statements
- Excessive graphics
- Soft skill overload
- Unverified tool claims
- Buzzword stuffing

Clarity and structure win.

Resume Strategy for Career Changers

If transitioning from another field:

Translate — do not rewrite history.

Instead of:
"Managed compliance documentation."

Write:
"Aligned operational processes with regulatory and internal control requirements; collaborated with cross-functional teams to address audit findings."

Security language increases relevance.

Your goal is reducing perceived risk.

Cover Letter Strategy (Modern Approach)

Cover letters are not mandatory — but when used correctly, they can differentiate you.

Keep it focused on:

- Why this role
- Why this organization
- What structured steps you have taken to prepare

Avoid long personal narratives.

One page maximum.

Final Strategic Guidance

A strong cybersecurity resume:

- Targets one role at a time
- Shows structured progression
- Demonstrates applied capability
- Uses precise language
- Avoids exaggeration

Competition is strong — especially at entry-level.

The candidates who stand out:

1. Align certifications with a role
2. Document hands-on capability
3. Present clearly and professionally

In the next chapter, we will examine how to strengthen your online presence — particularly LinkedIn positioning — to increase visibility and recruiter engagement.

8 Building Your LinkedIn Profile & Personal Brand

In modern cybersecurity hiring, your LinkedIn profile is not optional.

Recruiters, hiring managers, and security leaders routinely evaluate candidates online before interviews.

Your LinkedIn presence should reinforce the positioning established in your resume — not contradict it.

This chapter focuses on signal strength, not social media popularity.

Understanding LinkedIn's Role in Cybersecurity Hiring

LinkedIn serves three primary functions:

1. Recruiter discovery
2. Professional credibility review
3. Network-based opportunity flow

A strong profile increases visibility.
A weak or generic profile reduces credibility.

Your goal is clarity and consistency.

Align Your Profile to a Career Lane

Just as your resume must target a role, your LinkedIn headline must reflect your intended lane.

Avoid vague headlines like:

"Cybersecurity Enthusiast"
"Open to Opportunities"

Instead, position intentionally:

- "Entry-Level SOC Analyst | Cloud-Aware Defense | CC & Cloud+ Certified"
- "GRC-Focused Security Professional | CC → Cloud+ → CGRC Pathway"
- "Early-Career Cybersecurity Professional | Hybrid Infrastructure & Risk Alignment"

Specificity signals direction.

Crafting a Strong Headline

Your headline should:

- Contain searchable keywords
- Reflect your target role
- Show progression

Avoid listing too many buzzwords.
Recruiters scan quickly.

Think: clear and focused.

Writing a Professional Summary (About Section)

Avoid overly emotional or generic language.

Instead of:
"Cybersecurity is my passion."

Write:

"Early-career cybersecurity professional focused on cloud-aware defense and structured risk management. Completed foundational certifications (CC, Cloud+) and built documented hybrid lab environments simulating enterprise logging, IAM configuration, and vulnerability assessment workflows."

Show direction. Show action.

Avoid exaggeration.

Experience Section Strategy

LinkedIn allows more narrative detail than a resume.

Use it to:

- Expand on lab environments
- Describe frameworks studied
- Outline applied scenarios
- Demonstrate structured thinking

Example:

"Developed hybrid cloud lab environment simulating enterprise architecture. Implemented IAM roles, multi-factor authentication, and vulnerability scanning procedures. Documented security configurations aligned to NIST control categories."

Avoid simply listing:
"Completed 20 TryHackMe rooms."

Depth builds credibility.

Skills Section Optimization

LinkedIn's skills section affects search visibility.

Add skills aligned to your career lane:

SOC Track:
- Log Analysis
- Incident Response
- SIEM Concepts
- Cloud Security Basics

GRC Track:
- Risk Assessment
- NIST Framework Familiarity
- Control Mapping
- Governance Processes

Avoid adding skills you cannot explain in conversation.

Recommendations Matter More Than Likes

A thoughtful recommendation from:

- A mentor
- A manager
- An instructor
- A project collaborator

adds credibility.

One strong recommendation outweighs dozens of generic endorsements.

What to Post (High-Signal Content)

Posting daily is unnecessary.
Posting intentionally is powerful.

High-signal posts include:

- Explaining how a recent breach illustrates a specific control failure
- Sharing structured lessons learned from building a lab environment
- Analyzing a cloud misconfiguration case
- Reflecting on framework implementation challenges

Low-signal posts include:

• "Just passed Security+!" with no insight
• Generic cybersecurity memes
• Overly dramatic threat commentary

Demonstrate thinking — not noise.

Commenting Strategy (Underrated Visibility Tool)

Thoughtful comments often generate more credibility than original posts.

Instead of:
"Great post!"

Write:

"Interesting breakdown of identity misconfiguration risk. It highlights why IAM role scoping and least privilege reviews are critical in hybrid environments."

That signals understanding.

Networking the Right Way

Networking is not collecting random connections.

It is building professional alignment.

When sending connection requests:

• Personalize briefly
• Reference shared interest
• Avoid asking for a job immediately

Example:

"Hello [Name], I'm currently developing my skills in cloud-aware SOC operations and noticed your experience in hybrid security environments. I'd appreciate connecting and learning from your insights."

Short. Professional. Respectful.

Messaging Recruiters

If messaging a recruiter:

- Be concise
- Mention the specific role
- Highlight relevant credentials
- Avoid attaching your life story

Example:

"Hello [Name], I recently applied for the SOC Analyst position at [Company]. My background includes CC and Cloud+ certifications and documented cloud lab experience. I'd appreciate any additional insight into the role."

Professional. Direct.

Using LinkedIn as a Discovery Engine

Enable "Open to Work" (Recruiter-only visibility if preferred).

Follow:

- Security vendors
- Consulting firms
- Federal contractors
- Cloud providers
- Compliance-focused organizations

Many opportunities circulate through network activity before formal postings.

Building Professional Signal Beyond LinkedIn

LinkedIn is one channel. Your professional signal can also include:

- GitHub repositories
- Technical blog posts
- Published lab documentation
- Security writeups
- Participation in community forums

Your digital footprint should reinforce:

Structured thinking
Applied skill
Professional tone

Personal Branding in Cybersecurity (Realistic Framing)

Personal branding does not mean:

- Acting like an expert prematurely
- Posting constantly
- Manufacturing authority

It means:

- Demonstrating consistent development
- Communicating clearly
- Aligning your online presence with your target role

In competitive markets, quiet credibility outperforms loud enthusiasm.

Final Thoughts

Your LinkedIn profile should:

- Mirror your resume positioning
- Reflect your chosen lane
- Demonstrate applied learning
- Signal professionalism

Recruiters increasingly evaluate both skill and maturity.

Clarity, structure, and credibility create opportunity.

In the next chapter, we will examine structured networking, mentorship, and professional relationship building beyond social platforms.

9 Networking, Trust, and Professional Credibility

In cybersecurity, relationships influence opportunity — but not in the way most people assume.

Networking is not about collecting contacts.
It is about building professional credibility.

Referrals, mentorships, and hidden job opportunities emerge when other professionals view you as capable, serious, and trustworthy.

This chapter focuses on trust-building — not transactional networking.

Understanding the Hidden Job Flow

Many cybersecurity roles are filled through:

- Internal referrals
- Manager recommendations
- Professional networks
- Former colleagues

Why?

Because hiring managers prefer reduced risk.

A referred candidate carries implied credibility.
A cold applicant carries uncertainty.

Networking reduces uncertainty.

But only when it is done correctly.

What Effective Networking Actually Looks Like

Effective networking is:

• Showing up consistently
• Asking thoughtful questions
• Demonstrating structured learning
• Following up professionally
• Contributing when possible

It is not:

• Asking strangers for jobs
• Sending mass connection requests
• Treating professionals as stepping stones

Reputation travels quickly in cybersecurity communities.

Professionalism matters.

Conferences and Events (Strategic Approach)

Industry events can be valuable — but only if approached intentionally.

Well-known events include:

• Black Hat
• DEF CON
• BSides
• RSA Conference
• ISC2 Security Congress
• Local ISSA, ISACA, OWASP chapter meetings

However, attending alone does not create opportunity.

To maximize value:

Before the event:
• Identify speakers or professionals you want to meet
• Prepare thoughtful questions
• Research the organizations represented

During the event:
• Ask focused, relevant questions
• Listen more than you speak
• Avoid dominating conversations
• Exchange contact information selectively

After the event:
• Send a brief follow-up message
• Reference the specific conversation
• Express appreciation

Professional follow-through separates serious candidates from casual attendees.

Online Networking (Beyond LinkedIn)

Online engagement is often more consistent and sustainable than conferences.

Ways to build credibility:

• Contribute meaningfully to discussions
• Offer structured perspectives on security topics
• Share documented lab projects
• Ask intelligent, specific questions

Avoid posting for attention.
Aim to demonstrate understanding.

Consistency builds familiarity.
Familiarity builds trust.

How Referrals Actually Happen

Referrals typically occur when:

- Someone has seen your work
- Someone has observed your professionalism
- Someone trusts your competence

Referrals are rarely given to:

- People who ask immediately
- People who show little effort
- People with inflated claims

The strongest referrals come from:

- Former supervisors
- Project collaborators
- Mentors who have seen your development
- Professionals you have consistently engaged with

Trust precedes recommendation.

Building Strong References

References matter most:

- After final interview rounds
- When hiring managers want validation
- In regulated or government environments

A strong reference can speak to:

- Your reliability
- Your analytical thinking
- Your integrity
- Your communication ability

Prepare your references.

Before listing someone:

- Ask permission
- Share the job description
- Explain the role you're pursuing

This allows them to tailor their comments effectively.

Weak references provide generic statements.
Strong references provide specific examples.

Mentorship (Realistic Approach)

Mentorship is valuable — but rarely formal at first.

Avoid cold messages like:

"Will you be my mentor?"

Instead:

- Ask specific, focused questions
- Demonstrate you've done prior research
- Apply advice and report back

Mentorship often develops organically when:

- A professional sees consistent effort
- You implement guidance
- You respect their time

Long-term professional relationships grow through mutual respect.

The Long-Term Value of Relationships

Cybersecurity is a relatively small community.

Your reputation will follow you.

Networking done well:

- Opens unexpected opportunities
- Provides industry insight
- Builds confidence
- Strengthens leadership potential

Networking done poorly:

- Damages credibility
- Creates transactional impressions
- Reduces trust

Optimize for long-term credibility.

Giving Back

As your career progresses:

- Share knowledge
- Assist newcomers
- Offer thoughtful guidance
- Recommend strong candidates

The cybersecurity field values reciprocity.

Today's learner becomes tomorrow's leader.

Final Thoughts

Networking is not about visibility.
It is about trust.

Referrals, mentorships, and opportunities emerge when:

- Your capability is visible
- Your professionalism is consistent
- Your engagement is thoughtful

Build relationships with integrity.
Invest in credibility.

In the next chapter, we will examine interview strategy — and how to communicate your capability clearly under pressure.

10 Mastering the Cybersecurity Job Interview

Cybersecurity interviews do not simply test knowledge.

They test:

• How you think
• How you prioritize risk
• How you communicate under pressure
• How you handle uncertainty

Technical knowledge matters — but structured reasoning differentiates professionals.

This chapter focuses on interview strategy, not memorization.

Understanding How Cybersecurity Interviews Are Structured

Most cybersecurity interviews follow a layered evaluation model:

1. Recruiter Screening
2. Technical Evaluation
3. Scenario-Based or Case Discussion
4. Behavioral and Cultural Assessment

Each stage tests something different.

Understanding that structure reduces anxiety and improves performance.

Stage 1: Recruiter Screening

This stage evaluates:

- Communication clarity
- Resume consistency
- Certification legitimacy
- Professional tone

You may be asked:

- Why are you interested in this role?
- Walk me through your background.
- What certifications do you hold?

Keep answers:

- Concise
- Structured
- Focused on your target lane

Avoid over-explaining.

Stage 2: Technical Evaluation

This stage tests:

- Foundational knowledge
- Conceptual clarity
- Practical reasoning

Common areas include:

- Networking fundamentals
- Encryption basics
- Identity and access management
- Incident response workflow

• Cloud security concepts
• Log analysis logic

Interviewers are not only checking if you know definitions.

They are evaluating whether you can explain concepts clearly and logically.

How to Answer Technical Questions Effectively

When asked a technical question:

1. Define the concept briefly.
2. Explain how it works.
3. Connect it to a real-world scenario.

Example:

"What is multi-factor authentication?"

Weak answer:
"It adds another factor."

Stronger answer:
"Multi-factor authentication requires two or more independent authentication factors — typically something you know, something you have, or something you are. It reduces risk by preventing credential-only compromise, particularly in phishing-based attacks."

Structured answers signal maturity.

Scenario-Based Questions (Most Important)

Modern interviews heavily use scenarios.

Examples:

• You detect unusual outbound traffic. What do you do?
• A ransomware attack begins spreading. What are your first steps?
• An executive resists a security control. How do you respond?

These questions evaluate:

• Prioritization
• Calm reasoning
• Communication ability
• Risk understanding

When answering scenarios:

1. Clarify assumptions.
2. Identify immediate containment steps.
3. Explain investigation steps.
4. Address communication and documentation.
5. Mention prevention improvements.

Think process — not panic.

What to Do If You Don't Know the Answer

You will not know everything.

Interviewers expect that.

If you are unsure:

• Acknowledge it honestly.
• Explain how you would approach solving it.
• Outline investigative steps.

Example:

"I'm not fully certain of that implementation detail, but I would begin by reviewing logs, validating configuration, and consulting documentation before applying changes."

Structured humility is better than guessing.

Behavioral Evaluation: Professional Maturity

Cybersecurity roles require:

• Team collaboration
• Clear documentation
• Calm response under stress
• Ethical decision-making

Expect questions like:

• Tell me about a time you handled pressure.
• Describe a difficult technical issue you resolved.
• Explain how you communicated a technical issue to non-technical stakeholders.

Use the STAR method:

Situation
Task
Action
Result

Focus on outcomes and learning.

Demonstrating Risk-Based Thinking

Security decisions are rarely binary.

Interviewers want to see that you understand:

• Risk prioritization
• Business impact
• Tradeoffs

Example:

If asked how to secure a cloud application:

Don't just list tools.

Explain:

- Identity controls
- Logging
- Encryption
- Access segmentation
- Backup strategy
- Monitoring

Show layered thinking.

Hands-On and Whiteboard Assessments

Some interviews may include:

- Log analysis exercises
- Architecture discussions
- Threat modeling
- Whiteboard design challenges

Preparation strategy:

- Practice explaining architectures aloud.
- Review common attack paths.
- Be comfortable diagramming simple environments.

During whiteboarding:

Think aloud.
Walk through assumptions.
Invite clarification.

Interviewers assess your reasoning — not artistic ability.

Questions You Should Ask

Strong candidates ask thoughtful questions.

Consider:

- How does this team handle incident escalation?
- What logging or monitoring tools are currently in use?

• What are the most common security challenges in this environment?
• How does the organization balance security with business velocity?

Asking strategic questions demonstrates seriousness.

Post-Interview Follow-Up

Within 24 hours:

Send a concise thank-you message.

Reference:

• A specific topic discussed
• Your appreciation
• Continued interest

Professional follow-up reinforces maturity.

Evaluating an Offer

If you receive an offer:

Evaluate:

• Compensation
• Learning opportunities
• Team structure
• Exposure to tools and frameworks
• Career growth

Early-career professionals should prioritize:

Learning velocity
Skill development
Environment quality

Negotiation should be professional, not confrontational.

Common Interview Mistakes

- Overstating experience
- Memorizing definitions without understanding
- Speaking negatively about former employers
- Failing to prepare structured answers
- Appearing defensive under questioning

Calm clarity outperforms performative confidence.

Final Thoughts

Cybersecurity interviews test thinking more than trivia.

To succeed:

- Understand foundational concepts
- Practice structured explanation
- Demonstrate risk awareness
- Communicate clearly
- Admit uncertainty responsibly

Every interview is practice.

Each one improves your reasoning, clarity, and confidence.

In the next chapter, we will examine long-term career growth — and how to evolve beyond your first cybersecurity role.

11 The First 90 Days in Your Cybersecurity Job

Landing your first cybersecurity role is not the finish line.

It is the beginning of your professional reputation.

Your first 90 days determine:

• Whether you are seen as dependable
• Whether you are trusted with responsibility
• Whether you are viewed as high potential
• Whether you blend in — or stand out

The goal of your first 90 days is not to be impressive.

The goal is to become reliable.

The Reality of the First 30 Days: Controlled Overwhelm

Your first month will feel like information overload.

New systems.
New terminology.
New workflows.
New acronyms.
New expectations.

This is normal.

What matters is how you handle it.

During the first 30 days, your primary objectives are:

• Understand the environment
• Learn how work flows through the team
• Observe how decisions are made
• Identify documentation sources
• Clarify escalation paths

Do not focus on "proving" yourself yet.

Focus on understanding the system.

Days 1–30: Learn Before You Lead

In the first month:

1. Map the Environment

Understand:

• What tools are used (SIEM, EDR, ticketing, cloud platform)
• What frameworks guide operations (NIST, ISO, CIS)
• How incidents are escalated
• Who approves security decisions
• Where documentation lives

Create your own personal operating notebook.

Not everything will be written down.

2. Study Past Incidents

Ask to review:

• Previous incident tickets
• Security alerts that escalated

• Post-incident reports
• Audit findings

Patterns matter.

The fastest way to understand your organization's real security posture is to examine what actually went wrong before you arrived.

3. Watch Senior Team Members Closely

Observe:

• How they investigate alerts
• How they prioritize
• How they communicate findings
• How they escalate issues

You are learning judgment — not just tool usage.

Days 31–60: Contribute With Discipline

By the second month, expectations shift.

You are no longer "just onboarding."

You are expected to contribute reliably.

Your focus becomes:

• Ticket accuracy
• Documentation quality
• Alert triage discipline
• Clear communication

This is where many new professionals either rise — or struggle.

Deliver Clean Work

Security teams value:

• Clear notes
• Structured ticket updates
• Proper evidence collection
• Concise summaries

When updating a ticket:

Instead of:
"Checked logs. Looks fine."

Write:
"Reviewed authentication logs from 14:00–16:00 UTC. No anomalous source IPs observed. No privilege escalation attempts detected. Marking as false positive."

Clarity builds trust.

Communicate Risk, Not Just Activity

Avoid saying:
"The vulnerability is present."

Say:
"The vulnerability allows remote code execution on externally facing systems. If exploited, it could impact customer data. Recommending patch within 48 hours."

Cybersecurity is about risk communication.

Learn this early.

Days 61–90: Establish Professional Identity

By month three, leadership begins evaluating:

• Can this person operate independently?
• Do they understand risk tradeoffs?
• Do they escalate appropriately?
• Can they be trusted in incidents?

Now is the time to:

- Suggest small improvements
- Ask deeper architectural questions
- Volunteer for a structured task
- Show ownership of a repeatable process

Do not attempt to redesign the environment.

Improve within your lane.

The Three Behaviors That Accelerate Growth

Across all cybersecurity roles, three behaviors consistently accelerate advancement:

1. Calm Under Pressure

Incidents will happen.

Respond:

- Structured
- Clear
- Evidence-based

Panic spreads. Calm stabilizes.

2. Documentation Discipline

If it is not documented, it did not happen.

Strong documentation:

- Protects you
- Protects the organization
- Reduces repeat errors
- Increases leadership confidence

This habit alone differentiates professionals.

3. Business Awareness

Pay attention to:

- What systems generate revenue
- What systems handle sensitive data
- What regulatory pressures exist
- What leadership worries about

Cybersecurity decisions are business decisions.

Understanding that early elevates you beyond entry-level thinking.

Integrating AI Into Your Workflow (Modern Reality)

Many security teams leverage AI tools for:

- Log summarization
- Threat intelligence correlation
- Policy drafting
- Report generation

Your responsibility is not to blindly trust AI.

It is to:

- Validate outputs
- Cross-check conclusions
- Understand underlying logic

Professionals who combine AI efficiency with human judgment outperform both pure automation and pure manual work.

Avoid These Early-Career Mistakes

Trying to Prove Yourself Too Quickly

Security is precision work.

Slow is smooth.
Smooth is fast.

Staying Silent When Confused

Ask early.
Clarify assumptions.
Prevent errors.

Overconfidence With Limited Context

You do not yet understand the political, historical, or technical complexity of the environment.

Be curious before being corrective.

Neglecting Work-Life Sustainability

Security can become 24/7 mentally.

Protect:

- Sleep
- Health
- Mental clarity

Burnout destroys promising careers.

Build a 12-Month Vision Early

Before day 90, ask yourself:

- What skill do I want to strengthen this year?
- What certification aligns with my role?
- What area of the environment do I want deeper exposure to?

Align growth with your lane:

SOC Track:
Incident response depth → threat hunting exposure → cloud security awareness

Governance Track:
Control assessment mastery → documentation rigor → audit readiness support

Cloud Track:
IAM design → logging strategy → secure architecture review

Growth is intentional.

How Leadership Decides You're "High Potential"

Managers look for:

- Ownership
- Initiative within boundaries
- Clarity in communication
- Reliability under pressure
- Curiosity without ego

It is rarely about brilliance.

It is about trust.

Final Thoughts

Your first 90 days are not about being the smartest person in the room.

They are about becoming the most dependable person in the room.

Learn deliberately.
Communicate clearly.
Document precisely.
Think in risk.
Grow steadily.

The habits you build now compound across your entire cybersecurity career.

Your first role establishes professional foundation.

12 Long-Term Success in Cybersecurity

Breaking into cybersecurity is an achievement.

But it is not the destination.

It is the doorway.

Many professionals spend years trying to "get in."
Few spend time thinking about what happens after they do.

The reality is this:

Cybersecurity is not just a job market.
It is a profession.
And professions require evolution.

The threats will change.
The technology will shift.
The compliance landscape will tighten.
The cloud will expand.
Artificial intelligence will accelerate both defense and attack.

The question is not whether cybersecurity will change.

The question is whether you will change with it.

From Entry-Level Professional to Industry Contributor

Early in your career, success is defined by acquisition.

You acquire:

- Skills
- Certifications
- Experience
- Exposure

You learn how tools function.
You learn how incidents unfold.
You learn how organizations actually operate — not how textbooks describe them.

But eventually, the metric changes.

You are no longer evaluated on what you are learning.

You are evaluated on what you are contributing.

This is where long-term success begins.

The Shift From Execution to Judgment

In your first years, you execute tasks:

Review logs.
Escalate tickets.
Document findings.
Apply patches.

Over time, you begin making decisions.

Is this alert noise — or signal?
Is this vulnerability urgent — or manageable?
Is this control worth the operational friction it introduces?

Judgment becomes your currency.

And judgment is built through repetition, reflection, and humility.

The professionals who advance are not those who memorize the most acronyms.

They are those who develop sound decision-making under uncertainty.

Specialization Without Isolation

As your career progresses, you will feel pressure to specialize.

That is appropriate.

Security operations, cloud security, governance and risk, architecture, penetration testing — each demands depth.

But there is a danger in becoming too narrow.

The strongest cybersecurity professionals develop T-shaped expertise:

Deep in one area.
Broad across many.

A SOC analyst who understands cloud identity.
A GRC professional who understands technical control implementation.
A cloud engineer who understands regulatory exposure.

Breadth keeps you relevant.
Depth makes you valuable.

You need both.

The Risk Translation Skill

One of the most important abilities for long-term success is something rarely taught in certification courses:

Risk translation.

The ability to take technical findings and convert them into business implications.

Early-career professionals say:
"The server is missing patches."

Mid-career professionals say:
"The unpatched system increases exposure to remote exploitation."

Senior professionals say:
"If exploited, this system could interrupt customer transactions and expose regulated data, creating financial and reputational impact."

Same technical issue.
Different career levels.

If you want longevity, learn to speak the language of consequence.

Staying Relevant in a Rapidly Evolving Field

Cybersecurity does not allow stagnation.

The threats evolve.
The infrastructure evolves.
The attack surface expands.

Ransomware matured from crude encryption to double extortion models.
Cloud misconfigurations now account for significant breach vectors.
AI tools are being used for both phishing campaigns and defensive automation.
Identity has become the new perimeter.

Long-term success requires constant recalibration.

Not panic.

Not obsession.

Recalibration.

Schedule time to:

- Study emerging attack patterns
- Review new architectural models
- Understand regulatory changes
- Explore evolving tooling

Curiosity must remain active.

The Role of Cloud and Identity in Career Durability

If there is one reality shaping modern cybersecurity careers, it is this:

Everything is becoming cloud-centric and identity-driven.

Infrastructure is abstracted.
Networks are dissolving.
Applications are distributed.
Access is identity-based.

Whether you are technical or governance-focused, understanding:

- IAM (Identity and Access Management)
- Cloud logging
- API exposure
- Privileged access controls
- Zero Trust principles

is no longer optional.

Professionals who ignore cloud evolution limit their trajectory.

Professionals who understand cloud risk remain indispensable.

Leadership Is a Skill, Not a Promotion

Many assume leadership begins with title.

In cybersecurity, leadership begins with influence.

It begins when:

- Colleagues seek your input
- Management trusts your summaries
- Incidents calm down when you enter the room
- Decisions reflect your recommendations

Leadership skills include:

- Emotional control under pressure
- Clear and concise communication
- Accountability
- Strategic thinking
- Resource prioritization

Technical brilliance without communication clarity rarely scales.

Influence multiplies impact.

Moving Toward Executive Roles

If your goal is to eventually move into executive security leadership — Director, VP, CISO — your growth must shift.

Technical mastery becomes assumed.

Strategic fluency becomes required.

Case Example: Ten-Year Executive Trajectory

A mid-level Security Engineer earning $98,000 began intentionally repositioning toward governance and enterprise risk. In year one, he earned CISSP and began participating in internal risk review meetings. By year three, he transitioned into a Security Architect role at $135,000, expanding responsibility to cloud security design and control mapping across business units.

Between years four and six, he led a zero-trust implementation initiative and began presenting risk summaries to executive leadership. He completed CISM and later CCRMP, strengthening his risk quantification and governance depth. Compensation increased to $165,000 as Director of Security Architecture.

By year eight, he was responsible for enterprise security strategy across multiple cloud environments, managed a team of twelve, and owned a multimillion-dollar security budget. In year ten, he accepted a CISO role within a regulated healthcare organization at $235,000 base compensation with performance incentives tied to risk reduction metrics and audit outcomes.

The trajectory was not driven by technical brilliance alone. It was driven by structured skill stacking, governance literacy, executive communication, and deliberate exposure to business-level decision-making.

You must understand:

- Budget constraints
- Regulatory exposure
- Legal implications
- Insurance considerations
- Board-level reporting
- Organizational politics

Security leaders do not only defend systems.

They align risk decisions with business tolerance.

This requires business literacy, not just security expertise.

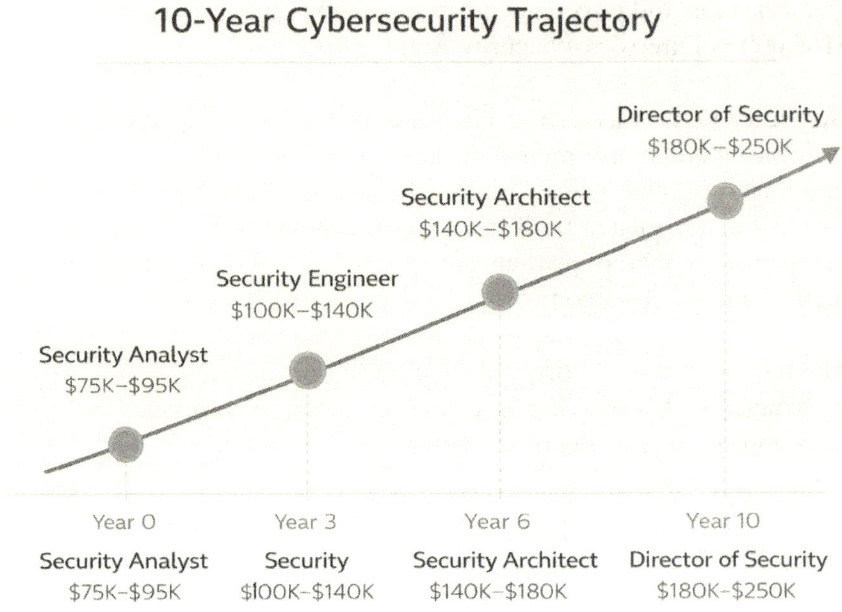

Figure 8. 10-Year Cybersecurity Trajectory

Avoiding the Burnout Cycle

Cybersecurity is demanding.

Incidents happen at inconvenient times.
Regulatory deadlines compress timelines.
New vulnerabilities surface without warning.

Many promising professionals leave the field not because they lack skill — but because they lack sustainability.

Long-term success requires:

- Setting boundaries
- Managing stress
- Preserving sleep
- Taking breaks
- Avoiding identity fusion with crisis

You are more effective calm than constantly reactive.

Longevity is an advantage.

The Power of Giving Back

One of the most underrated accelerators of long-term success is contribution.

When you:

- Mentor newcomers
- Write technical summaries
- Teach internal workshops
- Volunteer with professional organizations

you reinforce your own understanding.

Teaching clarifies thinking.

Mentorship builds influence.

Community involvement expands opportunity.

The cybersecurity community thrives on knowledge sharing.

Participation builds reputation.

Reputation builds resilience.

Building a 10-Year Vision

Most professionals think in six-month increments.

Few think in decades.

Ask yourself:

Where do I want to sit in ten years?

Still deeply technical?
Leading architecture decisions?

Managing security teams?
Advising executive leadership?
Consulting independently?

Your long-term path determines:

- Certification alignment
- Skill investment
- Networking strategy
- Professional branding

Intentional careers outperform accidental ones.

The Compound Effect of Professional Discipline

Careers compound the same way investments do.

Small habits accumulate:

- Clean documentation
- Clear communication
- Thoughtful risk assessment
- Continuous learning
- Professional reliability

Individually, they seem small.

Over years, they define trajectory.

Cybersecurity rewards those who are consistently disciplined more than those who are occasionally brilliant.

The Professionals Who Thrive

The ones who thrive long-term:

Curiosity, humility, adaptability, and business awareness sustain long-term relevance.

They do not cling to outdated models.
They do not resist evolution.
They do not rely solely on certifications.

They think.

They adapt.

They translate risk.

They build trust.

And they remain students — even after decades.

Final Reflection

You began this journey wanting to break into cybersecurity.

You now understand:

- The market is competitive.
- Certifications are strategic tools.
- Networking matters.
- Interviews test judgment.
- Early-role discipline builds credibility.
- Long-term success requires evolution.

Cybersecurity is a risk management discipline embedded in every modern enterprise.

It is a responsibility.

You protect systems.
You protect data.
You protect organizations.
You protect people.

If you remain adaptable, disciplined, and committed to growth, your relevance will not expire.

And your career will not plateau.

It will compound.

Epilogue: The Work Is Worth It

When you first considered breaking into cybersecurity, you probably saw headlines.

"Massive talent shortage."
"Six-figure salaries."
"Exploding demand."

It sounded exciting.
Maybe even urgent.

But by now, you understand something deeper.

Cybersecurity is not an easy shortcut.
It is not a guaranteed fast track.
It is not a trend.

It is work.

It is responsibility.

It is discipline.

And that is precisely why it is worth pursuing.

Throughout this book, we've stripped away the hype.

You've seen that the entry-level market is competitive.
You've learned that certifications are tools — not tickets.
You've seen that networking matters.
You've learned that interviews test thinking, not memorization.
You've seen that the first 90 days shape your reputation.
You've learned that long-term success requires evolution.

Breaking into cybersecurity is not about luck.

It is about positioning.

It is about skill acquisition.

It is about strategic effort.

And most of all, it is about becoming someone who can be trusted.

Because that is what cybersecurity really is.

Trust.

Organizations trust you with:

Sensitive systems.
Customer data.
Intellectual property.
Operational continuity.
Regulatory exposure.

They trust you to stay calm during incidents.
To think clearly when others panic.
To document thoroughly.
To communicate honestly.
To prioritize risk intelligently.

That trust is earned.

And it compounds.

There will be moments in your career where you feel overwhelmed.

An incident escalates unexpectedly.
A vulnerability affects production systems.
An executive challenges your recommendation.
A certification exam pushes your limits.

In those moments, recall the responsibility inherent in the profession.

Behind every system is a human being.
Behind every database is a story.
Behind every breach is real impact.

Cybersecurity is not abstract.

It matters.

Over time, your role will evolve.

You will move from learning tools to guiding decisions.
From executing tasks to influencing strategy.
From responding to incidents to shaping prevention.

If you remain curious, disciplined, and adaptable, your relevance will not fade.

Technology will change.
Threats will evolve.
But judgment, integrity, and clarity will always be valuable.

The industry does not need more noise.

It needs more professionals who:

Think critically.
Communicate clearly.
Document thoroughly.
Act ethically.
Stay humble.

If you commit to those principles, you will not just “break into” cybersecurity.

You will build something lasting within it.

Years from now, you will look back at this moment — the moment you decided to take cybersecurity seriously.

The courses.
The labs.
The certifications.
The applications.
The interviews.
The first day on the job.

You will realize that the hardest part was not learning the material.

It was choosing to persist.

There is no finish line in cybersecurity.

Only progression.

Only growth.

Only evolution.

But that is what makes it powerful.

You are stepping into a field that defends systems, safeguards organizations, and protects people at scale.

That is meaningful work.

And meaningful work is worth the effort.

The framework is established.
Deliberate execution determines trajectory.
Your cybersecurity career advances from this point forward.

Appendix A: Cybersecurity Learning Resources

Cybersecurity is not a static body of knowledge.

It is an evolving discipline shaped by:

• Adversary innovation
• Cloud expansion
• Regulatory pressure
• Identity-centric architectures
• Artificial intelligence

This appendix is not a list of everything available online.

It is a curated starting point — organized intentionally.

Choose resources aligned with your career lane and learning stage.

Books: Foundational and Advanced Reading

General Foundations

Cybersecurity for Beginners – Raef Meeuwisse
A clear introduction to core security concepts and terminology.

Certified in Cybersecurity: A Starting Point – Rob Chubbuck
A structured roadmap for understanding cybersecurity domains and certification strategy.

Mastering CISSP: A Comprehensive Guide to First-Time Exam Success – Rob Chubbuck

A domain-aligned deep dive for professionals advancing toward leadership or architecture roles.

Web Application Security & Offensive Foundations

The Web Application Hacker's Handbook – Stuttard & Pinto
A comprehensive breakdown of modern web vulnerabilities.

The Hacker Playbook 3 – Peter Kim
Practical penetration testing methodology aligned with real-world red team operations.

Hacking: The Art of Exploitation – Jon Erickson
Classic technical foundation for understanding exploit mechanics.

Blue Team, Detection & Incident Response

The Blue Team Handbook – Don Murdoch
Operational reference for SOC analysts and incident responders.

Applied Incident Response – Steve Anson
Structured IR methodology grounded in real-world casework.

Practical Malware Analysis – Sikorski & Honig
For those pursuing reverse engineering and malware dissection.

Governance, Risk & Compliance (GRC) Track

Governance, Risk, and Compliance is not "less technical" security.

It is structured risk translation.

GRC professionals ensure that security controls:

- Align with regulatory requirements
- Support organizational risk tolerance
- Are documented, assessed, and defensible
- Map to recognized frameworks

If you are pursuing the Governance Track (CC → Cloud+ → CGRC → CCRMP), your reading and study should reflect increasing depth in structured risk management.

Foundational Governance Reading

CISSP All-in-One – Shon Harris & Fernando Maymi
Broad coverage of enterprise governance, policy, risk, and security management concepts.

Certified in Cybersecurity: A Starting Point – Rob Chubbuck
Introduces core principles that form the baseline for structured governance and control understanding.

Intermediate Governance Depth

Mastering the CGRC: A Comprehensive Guide to Cybersecurity Using the Risk Management Framework – Rob Chubbuck

Designed for professionals moving into structured governance roles, this guide focuses on:

- NIST Risk Management Framework (RMF)
- Security control selection and tailoring
- System categorization (FIPS 199)
- Assessment procedures
- Authorization processes
- Continuous monitoring

This book bridges foundational security knowledge into formal compliance execution.

Ideal for professionals preparing for:

- CGRC certification
- Federal compliance roles
- Assessment and authorization environments

Advanced Governance & Risk Leadership

Mastering the CCRMP: A Comprehensive Guide to Cybersecurity Using the Risk Management Framework – Rob Chubbuck

Built for professionals who want to move beyond compliance into strategic risk leadership.

This text emphasizes:

- Enterprise risk alignment
- Organizational risk posture
- Governance program design
- Audit readiness strategy
- Executive risk communication
- Control maturity evolution

It is designed for professionals seeking to:

- Lead GRC programs
- Manage compliance initiatives
- Support executive-level security governance
- Transition toward Director or CISO-level strategy

Framework Documentation (Primary Sources)

Every serious GRC professional should read framework documentation directly:

- NIST SP 800-37 (Risk Management Framework)
- NIST SP 800-53 (Security Controls)
- NIST SP 800-171 (CUI protection requirements)
- NIST Cybersecurity Framework (CSF)
- ISO/IEC 27001 Annex A controls

Framework fluency is more valuable than exam memorization.

Practical Skill Development for GRC

Unlike technical tracks, GRC hands-on work looks like:

- Writing control narratives
- Mapping controls to frameworks
- Drafting security policies
- Conducting mock risk assessments
- Reviewing audit findings
- Performing gap analysis

Practice translating:

Control language → Business risk
Technical findings → Executive impact

This skill defines governance leadership.

Why Governance Professionals Become Organizational Multipliers

Governance professionals become organizational multipliers because they amplify the effectiveness of every technical team around them. A skilled GRC leader ensures that engineering teams build controls aligned to frameworks, that operations teams document defensible procedures, and that executives understand risk exposure in measurable terms. Rather than operating within a single technical domain, governance professionals connect security strategy to business continuity, legal requirements, financial planning, and enterprise architecture.

This multiplier effect is powerful. When governance is mature, audits are smoother, incidents are managed with documented authority, and security investments align directly to risk reduction. The governance professional does not just execute tasks—they shape how the organization thinks about risk. That influence extends across departments and increases enterprise resilience at scale.

Strategic Certification Alignment for Governance Track

Entry Level:
CC → Security+ → Cloud+

Mid-Level:
CGRC → CISA

Advanced:
CCRMP → CISSP → CISM

Certifications should align with increasing responsibility — not just resume stacking.

Blogs and Threat Intelligence Sources

These are not casual reading blogs.
They provide strategic insight.

Krebs on Security
Investigative reporting on breaches and cybercrime economics.

Schneier on Security
Security policy, cryptography, and risk philosophy.

Dark Reading
Enterprise-focused security trends and operational issues.

SANS Internet Storm Center
Daily technical threat analysis and incident breakdowns.

The Hacker News
Quick updates on vulnerabilities and emerging attacks.

Podcasts for Ongoing Awareness

Use podcasts for exposure, not primary study.

Darknet Diaries
Narrative exploration of real-world breaches and cybercrime cases.

CyberWire Daily
Concise cybersecurity news summaries.

Risky Business
Industry-focused conversations and strategic analysis.

Unsupervised Learning – Daniel Miessler
AI, security, and technology trend intersections.

Hands-On Platforms (Choose Based on Lane)

SOC / Detection Track

- TryHackMe
- CyberDefenders
- Blue Team Labs Online

Focus on:
- Log analysis
- Threat hunting
- Incident workflows

Offensive / Red Team Track

- Hack The Box
- PortSwigger Web Security Academy
- Offensive Security labs

Focus on:
- Web exploitation
- Privilege escalation
- Active Directory attack paths

Governance / Risk Track

Hands-on here means:

- Reviewing control frameworks
- Writing sample policies
- Practicing risk assessments
- Studying compliance reports

Resources:

• NIST CSF
• NIST RMF documentation
• CISA guidance
• OWASP Top 10 (for control alignment)

Cloud & Identity Track

Cloud literacy is no longer optional.

Study:

• AWS Well-Architected Framework (Security Pillar)
• Azure Security documentation
• Google Cloud security best practices

Understand:

• IAM policies
• Privileged identity management
• Logging and monitoring
• API security

Threat Intelligence and Research Tools

These tools are widely used in operational environments.

MITRE ATT&CK
Framework for mapping adversary behavior.

VirusTotal
File and URL reputation analysis.

CISA
Government advisories and security alerts.

NIST Cybersecurity Framework
Structured risk management guidance.

Certification Preparation Resources

Use these strategically — not endlessly.

Professor Messer
Strong foundational content for CompTIA certifications.

SANS Cyber Aces
Free fundamentals training.

Cybrary / Infosec Skills
Structured course-based study.

Reddit (r/cybersecurity)
Community insight — use critically.

How to Use This Appendix

Do not attempt to consume everything.

Instead:

If you are entry-level → focus on fundamentals and one hands-on platform.

If you are SOC-focused → emphasize detection labs and ATT&CK framework study.

If you are governance-focused → emphasize NIST documentation and risk modeling.

If you are cloud-focused → prioritize IAM and cloud logging architecture.

Curate your learning.
Avoid overwhelm.

Final Note

Cybersecurity knowledge compounds.

You do not need every resource.

You need consistency.

Choose intentionally.
Study deliberately.
Apply practically.

The professionals who stay relevant are not the ones who read the most.

They are the ones who connect knowledge to action.

Appendix B: List of Free and Paid Cybersecurity Training Platforms

Cybersecurity is built through repetition and applied understanding.

Access to training platforms has never been greater. But access does not equal progress.

The professionals who grow fastest are not the ones who join the most platforms — they are the ones who use platforms intentionally.

This appendix organizes training resources by:

• Cost structure (Free / Freemium / Paid)
• Career lane alignment
• Learning maturity

Choose deliberately. Complete fully. Advance strategically.

Free Cybersecurity Training Platforms

Free platforms are ideal for:

• Beginners building foundations
• Career changers testing interest
• Professionals reinforcing core skills

Cybrary

https://www.cybrary.it

Structured courses covering:

- Security fundamentals
- SOC operations
- Cloud security
- Certification preparation

Best used for foundational theory reinforcement.

TryHackMe

https://tryhackme.com

Hands-on labs covering:

- Networking fundamentals
- Linux basics
- Active Directory security
- Blue teaming
- Ethical hacking

Excellent starting point for SOC and Offensive track learners.

Hack The Box

https://www.hackthebox.com

More advanced hands-on labs focused on:

- Penetration testing
- Exploit chaining
- Privilege escalation
- Red team simulations

Best for intermediate to advanced learners.

Open Security Training

http://opensecuritytraining.info

Free deep technical content on:

• Malware analysis
• Reverse engineering
• Exploit development
• System internals

Ideal for those wanting low-level security depth.

Stanford Cryptography (Coursera – Audit Free)

https://www.coursera.org

University-level cryptography fundamentals.

Strong for identity and encryption depth.

FedVTE

https://fedvte.usalearning.gov

Free U.S. government cybersecurity training.

Ideal for:

• Veterans
• Federal job candidates
• Government-aligned professionals

Freemium Platforms (Free + Paid Upgrades)

These platforms allow exploration before deeper investment.

INE

https://ine.com

Focus areas:

- Penetration testing
- Networking
- Cloud security

Well-suited for serious technical learners.

SANS Cyber Aces

https://www.cyberaces.org

Free foundational training developed by SANS Institute.

Excellent stepping stone toward advanced SANS courses.

Boson

https://www.boson.com

High-quality certification practice exams.

Best used when you are close to exam readiness.

Paid Cybersecurity Training Platforms

Paid platforms should align with defined career direction.

SANS Institute

https://www.sans.org

Industry-recognized advanced training in:

- Incident response
- Forensics
- Cloud security
- Penetration testing
- Governance

Often employer-sponsored due to cost.

Offensive Security

https://www.offsec.com

Advanced hands-on certifications including:

- OSCP
- OSWE
- OSEP

Highly respected in offensive security roles.

Pluralsight

https://www.pluralsight.com

Subscription-based technical training covering:

- Cloud security
- Malware analysis
- Scripting
- Certification prep

Good for structured IT-to-security transitions.

Coursera Cybersecurity Specializations

https://www.coursera.org

University-backed programs from:

- Stanford
- Google
- MIT
- IBM

Strong for governance and theoretical depth.

Udemy Cybersecurity Courses

https://www.udemy.com

Affordable tactical courses.

Quality varies — choose instructors carefully.

Structured Career Ecosystem Resource YouCanGetCertified.com

https://www.youcangetcertified.com

A structured cybersecurity certification preparation and career acceleration platform designed to support:

- ISC2 CC
- CompTIA Cloud+
- CGRC
- CISSP
- Governance and risk development

Best for:

- Learners seeking guided certification pathways
- Professionals aligning study with career lanes
- Individuals who prefer structured progression over fragmented learning

It complements hands-on lab platforms by providing:

- Structured domain learning
- Practice question engines
- Certification-aligned progression paths

Use it as part of a deliberate certification roadmap, not as a replacement for hands-on skill development.

Career Lane Platform Alignment

Your platform selection should reflect your direction.

SOC / Detection Track

Primary Platforms:

• TryHackMe – https://tryhackme.com
• Blue Team Labs Online – https://www.blueteamlabs.online
• CyberDefenders – https://cyberdefenders.org

Focus on:

• Log analysis
• MITRE ATT&CK mapping
• Incident triage
• Threat hunting

Offensive / Red Team Track

Primary Platforms:

• Hack The Box – https://www.hackthebox.com
• Offensive Security – https://www.offsec.com
• PortSwigger Web Security Academy – https://portswigger.net/web-security

Focus on:

• Web exploitation
• Active Directory attacks
• Privilege escalation
• Exploit methodology

Governance / Risk Track

Hands-on work looks different here.

Practice through:

- NIST documentation – https://csrc.nist.gov
- NIST Cybersecurity Framework – https://www.nist.gov/cyberframework
- CISA guidance – https://www.cisa.gov

Pair with structured certification study such as:

- CGRC
- CCRMP
- CISSP

Governance mastery requires:

- Risk translation
- Control mapping
- Audit interpretation
- Executive communication

Cloud & Identity Track

Use vendor documentation and free tiers:

- AWS Security – https://aws.amazon.com/security
- Microsoft Azure Security – https://learn.microsoft.com/azure/security
- Google Cloud Security – https://cloud.google.com/security

Focus on:

- IAM
- Logging
- Privilege boundaries
- Zero Trust principles

Cloud and identity security significantly increase long-term career durability.

Avoiding Platform Overload

The greatest risk is fragmentation.

Joining five platforms and completing none builds confusion.

Instead:

Choose one primary platform.
Complete structured paths.
Apply knowledge in labs.
Document what you learn.
Advance deliberately.

Depth outperforms distraction.

Final Reflection

Cybersecurity training platforms are accelerators.

But they are not substitutes for:

Discipline
Consistency
Reflection
Application

Your growth will not be determined by the number of subscriptions you hold.

It will be determined by how deliberately you use them.

Choose wisely.
Commit fully.
Build steadily.

Appendix C: Sample Cybersecurity Resume and Cover Letter

A resume does not get you a job.

It earns you a conversation.

In cybersecurity, your resume must demonstrate three things immediately:

1. Technical competence
2. Business awareness
3. Measurable impact

Many candidates list tools.

Strong candidates demonstrate outcomes.

This appendix provides resume and cover letter examples — but more importantly, it teaches you how to position yourself at every stage of your cybersecurity career.

How Hiring Managers Read Cybersecurity Resumes

Recruiters scan resumes in 6–10 seconds.

Security managers look for:

- Certifications aligned to the role
- Relevant technical tools
- Quantifiable impact
- Clear progression
- Evidence of hands-on experience

If your resume reads like a lab report instead of a business document, it will not move forward.

Resume Structure Framework (All Career Levels)

Your resume should follow this structure:

1. Header (Contact + LinkedIn + GitHub if applicable)
2. Professional Summary (3–4 lines maximum)
3. Certifications (if relevant)
4. Core Skills (aligned to job description)
5. Professional Experience (impact-focused bullets)
6. Projects / Labs (if entry-level)
7. Education

Clarity > decoration.

The Power of Quantified Impact

Instead of:

- "Monitored SIEM alerts"

Write:

- "Monitored and triaged 250+ weekly SIEM alerts, reducing false positives by 18% through rule tuning."

Instead of:

- "Conducted vulnerability scans"

Write:

• "Performed monthly vulnerability scans across 400+ endpoints and reduced critical findings by 35% within six months."

Metrics demonstrate ownership.

Career Stage Positioning

Entry-Level Cybersecurity Resume Strategy

If you are new to the field:

You must compensate for lack of experience with:

• Labs
• Certifications
• Structured projects
• Volunteer or internship work

Your resume should emphasize:

• Security+ or CC
• Hands-on lab environments
• CTF participation
• Documentation ability

Do not hide home labs.

Document them professionally.

Example:

Home Security Lab – Self-Directed Project
• Built Active Directory lab environment using VirtualBox
• Simulated brute-force and phishing attacks
• Documented incident response process

Hiring managers respect initiative.

Mid-Level Resume Strategy (2–7 Years)

At this stage, your resume should reflect:

- Ownership
- Measurable improvements
- Cross-team collaboration
- Tool mastery

Remove beginner labs.

Focus on impact.

Example:

- Led cloud IAM restructuring project, reducing overprivileged accounts by 42%.
- Coordinated incident response during ransomware containment event, restoring operations within 12 hours.

You are no longer "learning."
You are delivering results.

SOC Track Resume Positioning

Highlight:

- Alert triage volume
- Threat classification
- MITRE ATT&CK familiarity
- Escalation handling

Example:

- Investigated 1,200+ security alerts per quarter using Splunk and CrowdStrike, escalating 3 confirmed high-severity incidents to IR team.

Show scale and maturity.

Governance / GRC Resume Positioning

This is often done poorly.

Avoid vague statements like:

• "Worked on compliance."

Instead write:

• Conducted NIST 800-53 control assessments across 75 systems.
• Developed POA&M documentation reducing audit findings by 28%.
• Led FIPS 199 categorization for moderate-impact system.

Governance resumes must show control literacy and documentation rigor.

If you hold:

CGRC
CCRMP
CISSP

Highlight framework familiarity.

Cloud Security Resume Positioning

Cloud roles require:

• IAM control
• Logging
• Configuration management
• Infrastructure as Code familiarity

Example:

• Implemented AWS CloudTrail monitoring and automated alerting via Lambda, reducing unauthorized API activity response time by 40%.

Cloud resumes must show automation awareness.

Leadership-Level Resume (Director / CISO)

At senior levels:

Remove tools.
Emphasize strategy.

Highlight:

- Budget oversight
- Security program development
- Board-level reporting
- Risk reduction metrics

Example:

- Built enterprise security roadmap aligned to NIST CSF, reducing critical vulnerabilities by 37% across 3-year transformation initiative.

Executives hire impact, not tool users.

Cover Letter Strategy

Your cover letter should:

- Be one page
- Reference the organization specifically
- Tie your experience to their risk profile
- Avoid repeating your resume

Strong cover letters do three things:

1. Show understanding of company security challenges
2. Highlight relevant strengths
3. Express strategic interest

Weak cover letters summarize the resume.

Cover Letter Psychology

Hiring managers subconsciously ask:

- Does this candidate understand our environment?
- Can they communicate clearly?
- Do they think like a security professional?

Answer those questions directly.

Example structure:

Opening: Why this company
Middle: Relevant impact + metrics
Closing: Alignment + enthusiasm

Applicant Tracking System (ATS) Optimization

Many cybersecurity resumes are filtered automatically.

To improve ATS performance:

- Mirror keywords from job descriptions
- Use standard headings (Experience, Skills, Certifications)
- Avoid excessive graphics
- Submit in PDF unless instructed otherwise

ATS systems scan for:

- Security tools
- Certifications
- Frameworks
- Years of experience

Strategic keyword alignment improves visibility.

LinkedIn Optimization

Your LinkedIn should reinforce your resume.

Include:

- Professional headline with specialization
- Certification listing
- Lab projects
- Articles or posts on cybersecurity

Example headline:

SOC Analyst | Threat Detection | MITRE ATT&CK | Security+ | Splunk | Cloud Fundamentals

Recruiters search LinkedIn aggressively.

Optimize for discoverability.

Portfolio Strategy (Highly Recommended)

Cybersecurity portfolios separate serious candidates from casual applicants.

Include:

- GitHub repositories
- Lab write-ups
- Redacted incident documentation
- Threat research summaries
- Risk assessment samples

Governance professionals can include:

- Sample risk registers
- Control mappings
- Mock audit findings

A portfolio proves capability.

Sample 1: Entry-Level Cybersecurity Analyst Cover Letter

John Doe
123 Cybersecurity Lane
New York, NY 10001
johndoe@example.com
(555) 555-5555
[Today's Date]

Hiring Manager
ABC Security Solutions
456 Technology Blvd
New York, NY 10001

Dear Hiring Manager,

I am excited to apply for the **Entry-Level Cybersecurity Analyst** position at ABC Security Solutions. With a **Bachelor's degree in Cybersecurity** from XYZ University and hands-on experience in security monitoring, vulnerability assessments, and incident response, I am eager to contribute my skills to your team.

During my cybersecurity internship at ABC Security Solutions, I monitored security events using SIEM tools, assisted in security audits, and researched vulnerabilities to strengthen organizational defenses. Additionally, I have built a home lab for hands-on practice with industry-standard security tools like Wireshark and Kali Linux.

My **CompTIA Security+ certification** demonstrates my commitment to industry best practices. I am passionate about threat detection, risk mitigation, and continuous learning in the ever-evolving cybersecurity landscape. I would love the opportunity to discuss how my skills align with your needs. Please feel free to contact me at your convenience.

Sincerely,
John Doe

Sample 2: Cybersecurity Engineer Resume (Mid-Level)

Sarah Smith
sarahsmith@example.com | (555) 555-5555 | LinkedIn: linkedin.com/in/sarahsmith | GitHub: github.com/sarahsec

Summary

Cybersecurity Engineer with **5+ years** of experience securing enterprise networks, conducting penetration tests, and implementing security controls. Strong background in **cloud security, incident response, and compliance (ISO 27001, NIST 800-53)**.

Skills & Tools

- Cloud Security (AWS, Azure)
- Penetration Testing & Vulnerability Management
- Identity & Access Management (IAM)
- Incident Response & Digital Forensics
- SIEM (Splunk, ELK)

Certifications

- Certified Ethical Hacker (CEH)
- AWS Certified Security – Specialty
- CompTIA CySA+

Experience

Cybersecurity Engineer – XYZ Tech Solutions | 2020 – Present

- Designed and implemented cloud security best practices for AWS and Azure environments.
- Conducted penetration tests to identify and remediate security vulnerabilities.
- Developed security policies and performed audits to maintain ISO 27001 compliance.

Sample 2: Cybersecurity Engineer Cover Letter

Dear Hiring Manager,

I am writing to apply for the **Cybersecurity Engineer** position at XYZ Tech Solutions. With over **five years of experience in penetration testing, cloud security, and incident response**, I am eager to bring my expertise to your security team.

In my current role at XYZ Tech Solutions, I led penetration testing initiatives, reducing system vulnerabilities by **35% over two years**. Additionally, I implemented **cloud security best practices** for AWS and Azure, enhancing compliance with ISO 27001 standards.

Holding **CEH and AWS Security certifications**, I am deeply committed to securing enterprise environments and continuously evolving my skills. I welcome the opportunity to discuss how I can contribute to your cybersecurity objectives.

Best regards,
Sarah Smith

Sample 3: SOC Analyst Resume

David Johnson
davidjohnson@example.com | LinkedIn: linkedin.com/in/davidjohnson

Summary

SOC Analyst with **2+ years** of experience in **threat monitoring, log analysis, and incident response**. Proficient in **Splunk, CrowdStrike, and Snort**, with hands-on experience in identifying and mitigating security threats.

Skills & Tools

- SIEM (Splunk, ELK)
- Network Traffic Analysis
- Threat Intelligence & Malware Analysis
- Endpoint Detection & Response (EDR)

Experience

SOC Analyst – CyberDefend Inc. | 2022 – Present

- Monitored security events across multiple platforms, analyzing and mitigating threats.
- Responded to **100+ security incidents**, collaborating with cross-functional teams.

Sample 4: Chief Information Security Officer (CISO) Resume

Michael Roberts
michaelroberts@example.com | (555) 555-5555

Summary

Seasoned **Chief Information Security Officer (CISO)** with **15+ years of experience** leading enterprise security strategies. Proven success in **risk management, compliance (NIST, GDPR), and cybersecurity governance**.

Key Achievements

- Built a security operations team, reducing security breaches by **40%**.
- Led enterprise **zero-trust implementation** across multi-cloud infrastructure.

Sample 5: Cybersecurity Consultant Cover Letter

Dear Hiring Manager,

With a passion for securing enterprise environments and **over 7 years of cybersecurity consulting experience**, I am excited to apply for the **Cybersecurity Consultant** position at XYZ Consulting Group.

Throughout my career, I have conducted **risk assessments, penetration tests, and security audits** for Fortune 500 clients. By implementing security frameworks such as **NIST and CIS Controls**, I have helped organizations strengthen their defenses against evolving cyber threats.

I would love to bring my expertise in **threat intelligence, vulnerability management, and compliance consulting** to your team. I look forward to discussing how my experience aligns with your needs.

Best regards,
[Your Name]

Sample 6: Governance, Risk, and Compliance (CGRC) Professional Resume

Emily Carter
emilycarter@example.com | (555) 555-5555 | LinkedIn: linkedin.com/in/emilycarter

Summary

Governance, Risk, and Compliance (GRC) professional with 6+ years of experience supporting federal and enterprise security programs. Experienced in NIST Risk Management Framework (RMF), control assessments, FIPS 199 categorization, and POA&M management. Skilled in aligning security controls with business objectives and regulatory requirements.

Skills & Tools

• NIST RMF (SP 800-37)
• NIST 800-53 Control Assessments
• FIPS 199 / FIPS 200
• Security Control Documentation & POA&M Development
• Risk Register Management
• Audit Support & Evidence Collection
• GRC Platforms (eMASS, Archer)
• Policy & Procedure Development

Certifications

- ISC2 Certified in Governance, Risk, and Compliance (CGRC)
- CISSP
- CompTIA Security+

Experience

Information Security Analyst (GRC) – SecureGov Solutions | 2020 – Present

- Conducted NIST 800-53 control assessments for moderate-impact federal systems.
- Developed and maintained System Security Plans (SSPs) and POA&Ms.
- Performed FIPS 199 categorization and supported Authority to Operate (ATO) processes.
- Coordinated with system owners to remediate audit findings and reduce high-risk vulnerabilities by 30%.

Compliance Analyst – TechRisk Consulting | 2018 – 2020

- Supported internal and external audits aligned with NIST and ISO 27001 standards.
- Mapped organizational controls to regulatory requirements.
- Assisted in risk assessments and documented mitigation strategies.

Sample 7: Cloud Security Engineer Resume

Daniel Thompson
danielthompson@example.com | (555) 555-5555 | LinkedIn: linkedin.com/in/danielthompson | GitHub: github.com/dthompsonsec

Summary

Cloud Security Engineer with 5+ years of experience securing AWS and Azure environments. Specializes in identity and access management (IAM), cloud monitoring, infrastructure hardening, and automation of security controls. Strong background in DevSecOps and cloud compliance frameworks.

Skills & Tools

- AWS Security (IAM, CloudTrail, GuardDuty, Config)
- Microsoft Azure Security Center
- Infrastructure as Code (Terraform, CloudFormation)
- Cloud Logging & Monitoring
- Container Security (Docker, Kubernetes)
- DevSecOps Practices
- Vulnerability Management

Certifications

- AWS Certified Security – Specialty
- CompTIA Cloud+
- CISSP

Experience

Cloud Security Engineer – CloudGuard Technologies | 2021 – Present

- Designed and implemented IAM least-privilege policies across multi-account AWS environment.
- Deployed automated CloudTrail monitoring and alerting to detect anomalous activity.
- Hardened containerized workloads and reduced misconfigurations by 40%.
- Integrated security testing into CI/CD pipelines to improve secure code deployment.

Security Engineer – DataSecure Inc. | 2018 – 2021

- Conducted cloud security assessments and remediated high-risk findings.
- Implemented encryption controls for data at rest and in transit.
- Supported compliance efforts for SOC 2 and ISO 27001 certifications.

Sample 8: Cybersecurity Compliance Analyst Resume

Laura Mitchell
lauramitchell@example.com | (555) 555-5555 | LinkedIn: linkedin.com/in/lauramitchell

Summary

Detail-oriented Cybersecurity Compliance Analyst with 4+ years of experience supporting regulatory compliance, risk assessments, and internal audit readiness initiatives. Proficient in NIST CSF, PCI-DSS, HIPAA, and ISO 27001 standards. Strong communicator with experience translating technical controls into business-aligned compliance documentation.

Skills & Tools

- NIST Cybersecurity Framework (CSF)
- PCI-DSS Compliance
- HIPAA Security Rule
- ISO 27001 Control Mapping
- Risk Assessments & Gap Analysis
- Policy & Procedure Documentation
- Audit Preparation & Evidence Review
- Vendor Risk Management

Certifications

- Certified Information Systems Auditor (CISA)
- CompTIA Security+
- ISO 27001 Lead Implementer (Training)

Experience

Cybersecurity Compliance Analyst – Enterprise Health Systems | 2021 – Present

- Conducted HIPAA security risk assessments and documented remediation plans.
- Led PCI-DSS gap analysis, reducing compliance findings by 25%.
- Assisted in internal audit preparation and evidence collection for annual ISO 27001 review.
- Developed security awareness documentation aligned with regulatory requirements.

IT Risk Associate – Compliance Advisory Group | 2019 – 2021

- Supported third-party risk assessments and vendor due diligence

reviews.
• Mapped technical controls to NIST CSF categories.
• Assisted in developing corporate security policies and governance documentation.

Final Thoughts

Your resume is not your autobiography.

It is your positioning document.

It must show:

Competence.
Clarity.
Impact.
Progression.

Every bullet should answer:

"What did this improve?"

Every cover letter should answer:

"Why you, for this company, right now?"

Cybersecurity hiring is competitive.

But it is also merit-based.

If you can demonstrate measurable value, aligned skills, and clear communication, you will stand out.

Build carefully.
Refine consistently.
Update quarterly.

Your resume should evolve as your career evolves.

Appendix D: LinkedIn Profile Checklist for Cybersecurity Professionals

LinkedIn is one of the most powerful professional tools available to cybersecurity practitioners. It functions as a digital resume, a networking platform, a recruiter discovery engine, and a credibility amplifier.

In cybersecurity, visibility and reputation matter. Recruiters frequently search LinkedIn before reviewing resumes. Some roles are never publicly posted and are filled entirely through recruiter outreach. If your profile is incomplete or poorly optimized, you will be invisible to opportunities aligned with your skills.

This appendix provides a structured narrative guide to optimizing your LinkedIn profile for cybersecurity roles at every stage of your career.

Professional Profile Picture

Your profile photo creates an immediate first impression. Use a clear, high-resolution headshot with proper lighting and a neutral background. Wear professional attire appropriate for cybersecurity roles, such as business casual or a blazer. Avoid casual event photos, heavy filters, group pictures, or distracting backgrounds.

Cybersecurity is built on trust. Your photo should reflect professionalism, clarity, and confidence.

Headline Optimization

Your LinkedIn headline is searchable and plays a major role in recruiter discovery. Avoid generic phrases such as "Cybersecurity Professional" or "IT Specialist." Instead, include keywords that reflect your specialization, tools, and certifications.

For example:

Cybersecurity Analyst | SIEM | Incident Response | Security+ | Threat Intelligence

Governance, Risk and Compliance (GRC) | NIST 800-53 | RMF | CGRC | Risk Management

Cloud Security Engineer | AWS | IAM | DevSecOps | Cloud+

Your headline should be concise, keyword-rich, and aligned with your target career track.

Banner and Visual Branding

Although often overlooked, your LinkedIn banner reinforces professional branding. Choose a clean, minimalist banner that subtly reflects cybersecurity themes or your professional focus. Avoid cluttered graphics or excessive text. Simplicity communicates maturity and focus.

About Section (Professional Summary)

The About section should clearly communicate who you are, what you specialize in, and where you are heading professionally. Keep it concise and structured in short paragraphs.

Begin with your professional identity and primary focus. Follow with key areas of expertise, frameworks, or tools. Conclude with certifications and career direction.

For example:

"I specialize in governance, risk, and compliance within enterprise and federal environments. My work centers on implementing the NIST Risk Management Framework, conducting control assessments, and supporting authorization processes. I hold CGRC certification and focus on aligning cybersecurity controls with organizational risk tolerance and business objectives."

Avoid copying your resume verbatim. This section should be strategic and forward-looking.

Custom LinkedIn URL

Claim a personalized LinkedIn URL that reflects your name and professional identity. Remove unnecessary numbers or random characters. A clean URL reinforces credibility and aligns with your resume and professional communications.

Experience Section

Your experience section must demonstrate measurable impact rather than listing responsibilities.

Instead of writing "Monitored SIEM alerts," write "Monitored and triaged over 200 weekly SIEM alerts, reducing false positives through detection rule refinement."

Instead of writing "Worked on compliance," write "Conducted NIST 800-53 control assessments and reduced high-risk findings by 30 percent through structured remediation planning."

Cloud professionals should highlight IAM improvements, logging enhancements, automation initiatives, and configuration hardening. Governance professionals should emphasize control assessments, documentation development, POA&M management, and audit support.

Quantified impact strengthens credibility.

Education and Certifications

Clearly list relevant degrees and certifications. Certifications significantly influence recruiter searches and filtering systems. Prominently display certifications such as Security+, Cloud+, CGRC, CISSP, CISM, or CISA where applicable.

Ensure certifications are current and aligned with your intended career path.

Skills Section

LinkedIn allows up to 50 skills. Prioritize technical skills aligned with your specialization and include relevant frameworks where appropriate.

Technical examples include SIEM, Incident Response, AWS Security, NIST 800-53, Vulnerability Management, and Zero Trust Architecture. Soft skills such as risk communication, analytical thinking, and leadership should also be included, particularly for governance and leadership roles.

Seek endorsements from colleagues or mentors to reinforce credibility.

Projects and Featured Section

The Featured section allows you to showcase professional artifacts. Entry-level professionals should include home lab documentation, GitHub repositories, or Capture the Flag participation. Governance professionals can include redacted risk assessments or control mappings. Cloud professionals may link to automation projects or architecture write-ups.

A visible portfolio demonstrates initiative and applied skill.

Community Engagement

Active engagement increases visibility. Follow cybersecurity leaders, organizations, and companies aligned with your career track. Comment thoughtfully on posts, share relevant articles, and occasionally publish insights about your learning journey.

Daily posting is unnecessary.

Strategic posting is effective. Consistency and substance are more important than volume. One meaningful post per week can significantly improve discoverability over time.

Security Clearance Positioning

If you hold a security clearance, list it appropriately without sharing sensitive details. For example, "Active Secret Clearance" is sufficient. Clearance status can significantly increase recruiter outreach in certain markets.

Recommendations

Request professional recommendations from supervisors, professors, mentors, or colleagues. Strong recommendations should reference specific achievements, tools, or frameworks and describe your reliability and professionalism.

Two to four well-written recommendations are generally sufficient.

Thirty-Day Optimization Plan

During the first week, update your headline, About section, and certifications. In the second week, refine your experience bullets to emphasize measurable impact and adjust your skills list. In the third week, add portfolio items to the Featured section and request recommendations. In the fourth week, begin consistent engagement through thoughtful comments or posts.

Incremental improvements compound over time.

Final Thoughts

LinkedIn is not merely a social platform. It is a professional positioning tool.

A strong LinkedIn profile increases recruiter visibility, reinforces resume credibility, builds authority, and expands networking opportunities. Cybersecurity is a reputation-driven industry, and your digital presence should reflect the discipline and expertise you bring to your work.

Build intentionally. Review quarterly. Update as your certifications, responsibilities, and achievements evolve.

Your professional brand should grow as your career grows.

Appendix E: Cybersecurity Interview Preparation Guidance

Preparing for a cybersecurity interview requires more than reviewing definitions or memorizing frameworks. Today's hiring environment demands a combination of technical competence, analytical reasoning, communication clarity, and professional maturity. Whether you are pursuing an entry-level SOC Analyst role, a penetration testing position, a Cloud Security Engineer opportunity, or an executive leadership position such as CISO, your preparation must be deliberate and strategic.

This appendix provides a structured roadmap to help you approach cybersecurity interviews with confidence and clarity.

Cybersecurity Interview Preparation Checklist

Pre-Interview Preparation

Before you ever enter the interview room—virtual or in person—you should:

- Research the company's security posture, industry focus, and threat landscape.
- Carefully review the job description and identify required skills, tools, and frameworks.
- Refresh your understanding of cybersecurity fundamentals, including networking, access controls, logging, and encryption.

- Practice answering both technical and behavioral questions out loud.
- Set up or review your home lab to reinforce hands-on skills.
- Prepare structured examples using the STAR method (Situation, Task, Action, Result).
- Review common security tools such as Splunk, Wireshark, Nmap, EDR platforms, or cloud security dashboards.
- Update your LinkedIn profile and resume so they align with the role.
- Prepare thoughtful questions to ask the interviewer.

Preparation is not optional—it is expected.

Step 1: Research the Company and Job Role

Before your interview, develop situational awareness about the organization.

You should understand:

- What industry they operate in (healthcare, finance, government, technology).
- Their likely regulatory obligations (HIPAA, PCI-DSS, GDPR, NIST frameworks).
- Whether they are cloud-native, hybrid, or on-premises.
- Whether they have experienced recent breaches or security events.
- What technologies they publicly reference (AWS, Azure, Splunk, Microsoft Defender, etc.).

For example, if you are interviewing for a SOC Analyst position at a company that uses Splunk, you should review:

- How logs are ingested and queried
- Basic search query syntax
- Alert triage processes
- False positive reduction strategies

Research transforms you from a candidate into a professional peer.

Step 2: Prepare for Technical Questions

Cybersecurity interviews typically include technical, scenario-based, and problem-solving questions.

Networking and Security Fundamentals

Be prepared to clearly explain:

- The OSI Model and TCP/IP model
- How firewalls differ from IDS/IPS
- The role of VPNs
- TLS versus SSL (and why SSL is deprecated)
- The differences between WAF and traditional firewalls

Clarity matters more than complexity. Interviewers evaluate your ability to communicate concepts effectively.

Threats and Attack Vectors

Expect questions such as:

- What is a man-in-the-middle attack?
- How does SQL injection work?
- What is cross-site scripting (XSS)?
- How does ransomware spread?
- What are common phishing techniques?

You will likely also encounter modern topics such as cloud misconfigurations, identity-based attacks, MFA bypass techniques, or credential stuffing.

Demonstrate reasoning, not memorization.

Incident Response and SOC Operations

Be ready to explain:

- The steps you would take if a user reports a phishing email
- The phases of incident response

- The difference between SIEM, EDR, and SOAR
- How to contain and isolate compromised systems

Employers want to see structured thinking under pressure.

Penetration Testing and Red Teaming

You may be asked:

- What is the MITRE ATT&CK framework?
- What vulnerabilities are included in the OWASP Top 10?
- How would you approach a penetration test engagement?
- What is the difference between vulnerability scanning and exploitation?

Focus on methodology and process.

Step 3: Master Behavioral Interview Questions

Technical skills alone are not enough. Behavioral questions often determine whether you receive an offer.

Cybersecurity professionals operate in high-pressure environments. Employers assess:

- Problem-solving ability
- Decision-making under stress
- Communication clarity
- Collaboration skills
- Ethical judgment

The most effective way to answer behavioral questions is by using the **STAR Method**.

The STAR Method Explained

The STAR Method structures your answers into four parts:

- **Situation** – Describe the context.
- **Task** – Explain your responsibility.

- **Action** – Detail what you did.
- **Result** – Share the measurable outcome.

This format keeps your responses clear, focused, and persuasive.

Example: Handling a Security Incident

Situation: While working as a Security Analyst, you identified unusual outbound traffic to an unknown external IP address.

Task: Your responsibility was to determine whether the activity was benign or malicious.

Action: You analyzed logs using Splunk, correlated endpoint data, identified compromised credentials, isolated the device, and blocked the IP at the firewall.

Result: The action prevented significant data exfiltration and led to enhanced phishing awareness training that reduced incidents by 30%.

Metrics add credibility.

Common Behavioral Question Themes

You may be asked to describe:

- A time you handled a security incident under pressure
- A situation where you identified and mitigated a risk
- A time you collaborated across departments
- A mistake you made and how you corrected it
- A technical concept you explained to non-technical stakeholders

When answering:

- Be specific
- Use measurable outcomes
- Keep responses concise (1–2 minutes)
- Highlight tools and frameworks used
- Demonstrate growth and learning

Employers hire professionals who reflect and improve.

Step 4: Prepare for Hands-On Assessments

Some organizations require practical demonstrations.

These may include:

- Analyzing SIEM logs
- Reviewing packet captures in Wireshark
- Solving Capture The Flag challenges
- Identifying vulnerabilities in a simulated environment

To prepare:

- Practice on platforms like TryHackMe or Hack The Box
- Review real-world attack case studies
- Build a simple home lab
- Practice writing incident summaries

Hands-on familiarity reduces stress and improves performance.

Step 5: Ask Thoughtful Questions

Strong candidates ask intelligent, business-oriented questions.

Examples include:

- What are the organization's biggest security challenges right now?
- How does the team measure success?
- What security frameworks guide your program?
- How does the company support ongoing professional development?
- How does the organization prioritize risk?

Your questions demonstrate strategic thinking.

Step 6: Post-Interview Professionalism

After the interview:

- Send a thank-you email within 24 hours.
- Reference a specific topic discussed.
- Reaffirm your interest and enthusiasm.
- Maintain a professional tone.

A concise follow-up reinforces maturity and attention to detail.

Final Thoughts: Cybersecurity Interview Success Strategy

Success in cybersecurity interviews is not accidental. It is the result of disciplined preparation.

Remember to:

1. Understand the company's security posture.
2. Review core technical foundations.
3. Practice structured behavioral responses.
4. Demonstrate measurable impact.
5. Prepare for practical assessments.
6. Follow up professionally.

In today's competitive hiring environment, preparation is your differentiator.

When you combine technical competence with structured communication and strategic awareness, you do more than answer questions—you demonstrate readiness.

Approach every interview as a security professional, not merely an applicant.

That distinction shapes perception.

Appendix F: AI-Era Cybersecurity Interview Questions

Artificial Intelligence is no longer a future topic in cybersecurity—it is embedded in today's operations. From AI-assisted phishing campaigns to machine learning-driven threat detection and AI coding copilots, modern security teams are navigating a fundamentally different environment.

Hiring managers now evaluate candidates not only on traditional security knowledge but also on their ability to operate in an AI-augmented landscape.

This appendix prepares you for the types of AI-era questions that are increasingly appearing in cybersecurity interviews.

Understanding the AI-Driven Security Landscape

Before diving into interview questions, understand the context:

- Attackers are using AI to generate phishing emails, deepfakes, and malware variants.
- Security teams are using AI for anomaly detection, automation, and alert prioritization.
- Developers are using AI coding assistants that introduce new security considerations.
- Organizations are concerned about data leakage through Large Language Models (LLMs).
- Governance teams are building AI risk management frameworks.

If you cannot speak intelligently about AI's impact on cybersecurity, you are not fully prepared for modern interviews.

Category 1: AI Awareness and Security Fundamentals

These questions assess your understanding of how AI intersects with cybersecurity.

Sample Questions

- How is artificial intelligence changing the threat landscape?
- What are the cybersecurity risks of generative AI tools?
- How can AI improve SOC operations?
- What risks do LLMs introduce to enterprise environments?
- How can attackers use AI for phishing or social engineering?

What Interviewers Are Looking For

They want to hear that you understand:

- AI lowers the barrier to entry for attackers.
- Phishing emails are more convincing due to generative text.
- Deepfake voice and video attacks are increasing.
- AI tools can accidentally expose sensitive data.
- AI can be used defensively for anomaly detection and automation.

Avoid generic answers. Show balanced thinking—both offensive and defensive implications.

Category 2: AI in Security Operations (SOC & Detection)

Security operations teams increasingly use machine learning and automation.

Sample Questions

- How can machine learning improve threat detection?
- What are the limitations of AI-driven detection systems?
- How would you validate an AI-generated alert?

- What risks exist when relying too heavily on AI automation?

Strong Answer Themes

- AI improves pattern recognition in large datasets.
- False positives remain a challenge.
- Human validation is still required.
- Bias in training data can impact detection quality.
- Over-automation can create blind spots.

Demonstrate critical thinking. AI is powerful—but not infallible.

Category 3: AI and Cloud Security

Cloud environments are increasingly integrated with AI services.

Sample Questions

- What are the risks of deploying AI models in the cloud?
- How would you secure AI APIs?
- What is model poisoning?
- What is prompt injection?

Key Concepts to Understand

- Data exposure through misconfigured storage.
- API key leakage.
- Prompt injection attacks manipulating model behavior.
- Model poisoning through corrupted training data.
- Access control and logging for AI systems.

If interviewing for Cloud Security roles, expect these topics.

Category 4: AI Governance, Risk, and Compliance (GRC)

Governance roles are seeing a major shift toward AI oversight.

Sample Questions

- How should organizations govern AI usage?

- What frameworks exist for AI risk management?
- What is responsible AI?
- How would you assess risk in deploying an internal AI tool?
- What controls would you recommend for AI systems?

Strong Response Themes

- AI systems require risk assessments.
- Data classification must apply to AI inputs.
- Audit logging of AI usage is essential.
- Human oversight is required.
- NIST AI Risk Management Framework awareness is valuable.
- Regulatory pressure is increasing globally.

Governance candidates should demonstrate structured risk-based thinking.

Category 5: AI Policy and Enterprise Controls

Organizations are now building policies around AI usage.

Sample Questions

- Should employees be allowed to use public AI tools?
- What risks exist when employees paste code into AI chatbots?
- How would you design an AI acceptable use policy?
- What is shadow AI?

Expected Knowledge Areas

- Data leakage risk.
- Intellectual property exposure.
- Compliance violations.
- Inconsistent AI outputs.
- Need for enterprise-approved AI platforms.
- Monitoring and logging AI usage.

Security professionals must balance innovation with control.

Category 6: AI-Assisted Development and DevSecOps

AI coding assistants introduce new risk vectors.

Sample Questions

- What risks come with AI-generated code?
- How would you validate AI-generated scripts?
- Can AI introduce vulnerable code patterns?
- How should DevSecOps adapt to AI copilots?

Strong Answer Components

- AI can generate insecure coding patterns.
- Secure code review remains essential.
- Static analysis tools should be applied.
- Developers must understand output—not blindly trust it.
- Governance must include AI code usage policies.

Demonstrate understanding of both development and security oversight.

Category 7: Ethical and Strategic AI Questions

Senior-level interviews may include broader questions.

Sample Questions

- Is AI making cybersecurity easier or harder?
- What ethical concerns surround AI in security?
- Should AI systems make autonomous security decisions?
- What risks do deepfake technologies present?

Professional-Level Insights

- AI accelerates both attackers and defenders.
- Human oversight must remain central.
- Autonomous decisions carry risk of misclassification.
- AI bias can impact investigations.
- AI-driven misinformation campaigns are increasing.

Show thoughtful, measured responses—not fear-based reactions.

AI-Focused Behavioral Questions

Modern interviews may blend AI and behavioral scenarios.

Examples:

- Tell me about a time you used automation to improve efficiency.
- Describe how you would respond if an AI tool produced incorrect output.
- How would you educate non-technical leadership about AI security risks?
- How would you implement AI governance in a growing organization?

Use the STAR method and emphasize structured thinking.

AI-Era Interview Preparation Strategy

To prepare effectively:

- Understand how attackers use AI.
- Understand how defenders use AI.
- Stay updated on AI governance developments.
- Learn basic terminology (LLM, prompt injection, model poisoning, hallucination).
- Develop balanced, critical responses.

You are not expected to be a machine learning engineer.

You are expected to understand risk.

Modern Hiring Reality

Hiring managers increasingly ask:

- How do you secure AI?
- How do you prevent AI misuse?

- How do you leverage AI responsibly?
- How do you balance innovation with control?

If you can answer these questions thoughtfully, you immediately differentiate yourself from candidates focused solely on legacy topics.

Final Perspective: AI as a Security Multiplier

Artificial Intelligence is neither inherently good nor inherently dangerous. It is a force multiplier.

For attackers, it increases speed and scale.
For defenders, it enhances detection and automation.

Security professionals who understand both sides—and can communicate risk clearly—will lead the next generation of cybersecurity programs.

Prepare accordingly.

Closing Thoughts: Your Career Begins Now

You are not simply pursuing a job in cybersecurity.
You are choosing to enter a profession responsible for safeguarding systems, data, infrastructure, and public trust.

That responsibility demands discipline, ethical judgment, structured learning, and long-term commitment.

If you have read this far, you are no longer exploring an idea. You are standing at the beginning of a deliberate professional path. Cybersecurity is not reserved for the naturally gifted or the mathematically elite. It rewards those who build skill methodically, think critically under pressure, and execute consistently over time.

Mastery in cybersecurity is iterative. Professionals refine, adapt, and recalibrate continuously as technologies evolve and threats shift. The individuals who succeed are not those who know everything — they are those who commit to continuous, structured growth.

The field needs disciplined professionals who can analyze risk, communicate clearly, and act decisively. Organizations are integrating artificial intelligence into authentication systems, fraud detection engines, vulnerability prioritization platforms, and automated security operations workflows. Cloud-native infrastructure is now standard architecture. Regulatory oversight is expanding across healthcare, finance, government, and critical infrastructure sectors. Boards of directors increasingly demand measurable risk reporting and accountable governance.

This convergence has created unprecedented demand for professionals who understand not only technical controls, but governance, compliance, operational resilience, and AI-related risk exposure.

If you build your foundation correctly, you will not merely enter the field — you will position yourself for leadership within it.

Your Next Strategic Moves

Now that you have a roadmap, your progress depends on execution.

1. Assess Your Current Position

Be honest and specific.

- If you are just beginning, focus on foundational knowledge and entry certifications such as ISC2 CC or CompTIA Security+. Build technical literacy before chasing specialization.
- If you have IT experience, identify the security discipline that aligns with your strengths — defensive operations, cloud security, governance and risk, penetration testing — and sequence certifications intentionally.
- If you are transitioning from another profession, leverage your transferable skills. Project management, documentation discipline, regulatory awareness, communication skills, and analytical thinking are assets in cybersecurity.

Clarity reduces wasted effort.

2. Sequence Certifications Strategically

Certifications should not be collected randomly. They should be sequenced deliberately.

If your goal is operational defense, your first 12–18 months may focus on:

CC → Security+ → Cloud+ → entry-level SOC or security operations role.

If governance, risk, and compliance align with your strengths, consider:

CC → Cloud+ → CGRC → compliance or risk analyst role.

Each certification should build toward responsibility, not just resume density.

Structured progression accelerates credibility.

3. Build Your Professional Infrastructure

Your cybersecurity career requires infrastructure just like any secure system.

- Optimize your LinkedIn profile to reflect measurable achievements.
- Build a home lab to gain hands-on experience.
- Participate in Capture The Flag challenges and simulation environments.
- Document your learning publicly when appropriate — blogs, GitHub repositories, technical summaries.

Cybersecurity hiring is often relationship-driven. Many roles are filled through referrals before public posting. Your professional network is not optional — it is strategic infrastructure for your career.

Engage intentionally.

4. Apply Before You Feel Ready

Perfectionism delays progress.

In cybersecurity, growth occurs on the job. You will not meet every qualification listed in a posting — and you do not need to. Apply for internships, entry-level roles, apprenticeships, and analyst positions once you have foundational competence.

Confidence grows through action.

5. Develop Discipline, Not Just Curiosity

Curiosity without structure leads to distraction.
Structure without consistency leads to frustration.

The professionals who advance are those who develop daily habits: reviewing logs, studying frameworks, practicing labs, refining documentation, analyzing case studies.

Your future income, influence, and responsibility will correlate directly with your discipline.

Professional Identity Matters

You are entering a field built on trust. Ethical conduct is non-negotiable.

Use security tools legally. Follow responsible disclosure practices. Respect privacy laws and compliance standards. Document your work thoroughly. Protect data as if it were your own.

Your reputation will follow you throughout your career. Guard it carefully.

Before You Close This Book

Answer these questions in writing:

1. What specific cybersecurity role am I targeting within the next 12 months?
2. What certification will I commit to completing in the next 90 days?
3. What measurable action will I take within the next 7 days?
4. Who will I contact for mentorship or professional connection this week?
5. What daily habit will I build to develop technical discipline?

Do not move on to another task until you write your answers.

The difference between aspiration and execution is disciplined documentation.

Final Perspective

Cybersecurity is not a short-term opportunity. It is a long-term profession.

The landscape will continue to evolve — AI risk governance, cloud-native defense strategies, regulatory accountability, automation of security operations, zero-trust architectures. The professionals who succeed will be those who combine technical literacy with governance awareness and clear communication.

Build correctly now to position yourself for influence, not just employment.

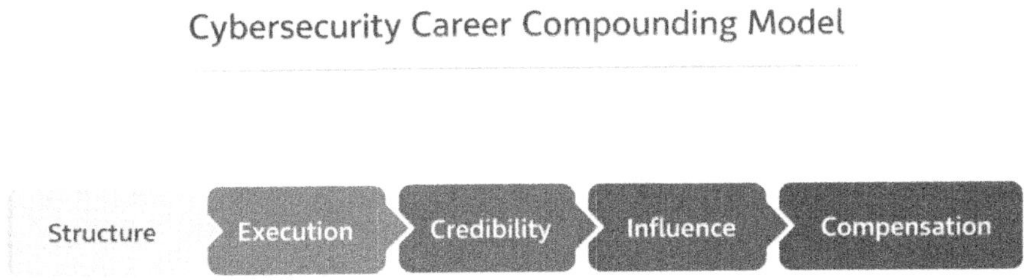

Figure 9. Cybersecurity Career Compounding Model

Your cybersecurity career will not be defined by luck.
It will be defined by the habits you build starting today.

Begin execution.

About The Author

Rob Chubbuck brings more than 25 years of cumulative experience in Information Security, Risk Management, and Enterprise Technology Architecture. Over the course of his career, he has supported small businesses, Fortune-level enterprises, and multiple U.S. Government programs, providing leadership in infrastructure design, system authorization, threat and vulnerability analysis, regulatory compliance, and enterprise security strategy.

Throughout his career, Mr. Chubbuck has mentored hundreds of IT and cybersecurity professionals who have advanced into senior engineering, governance, and executive leadership roles. His work spans network architecture, digital forensics, large-scale compliance programs, and federal system authorization initiatives.

He has extensive experience with enterprise security frameworks including the NIST Risk Management Framework (RMF), NIST Cybersecurity Framework (CSF), FedRAMP, HIPAA, and ISO/IEC 27001/27002. His advisory work includes control implementation, Authority to Operate (ATO) support, audit readiness preparation, disaster recovery planning, and enterprise risk alignment within regulated environments.

Mr. Chubbuck currently supports U.S. Government programs in the Washington, D.C. area, providing infrastructure and cybersecurity advisory services in mission-critical systems.

He holds a Master of Science in Information Security and Assurance and a Bachelor of Science in Information Technology. In addition, he maintains more than two dozen industry certifications, including CISSP, CCRMP, CEH, CHFI, EDRP, Security+, Network+, and others.

Mr. Chubbuck resides in the mountains of Western North Carolina.

Made in United States
North Haven, CT
31 August 2026

17732163R00114